# GOSPEL FOUNDATIONS

*GOD WITH US*

VOL. 5 | The Gospels

5

From the creators of *The Gospel Project*, *Gospel Foundations* is
a six-volume resource that teaches the storyline of Scripture. It is
comprehensive in scope yet concise enough to be completed in just one
year. Each seven-session volume includes videos to help your group
understand the way each text fits into the storyline of the Bible.

ISBN 9781535915557 • Item 005805890

Dewey decimal classification: 230

Subject headings: CHRISTIANITY / GOSPEL / SALVATION

Editorial Team

Ben Trueblood
*Director, Student Ministry*

JohnPaul Basham
*Manager, Student Ministry Publishing*

Andy McLean
*Content Editor*

Grace Pepper
*Production Editor*

Alli Quattlebaum
*Graphic Designer*

We believe that the Bible has God for its author; salvation for its end; and
truth, without any mixture of error, for its matter and that all Scripture
is totally true and trustworthy. To review LifeWay's doctrinal guideline,
please visit lifeway.com/doctrinalguideline.

To order additional copies of this resource, write to LifeWay Resources
Customer Service; One LifeWay Plaza; Nashville, TN 37234; fax 615-
251-5933; call toll free 800-458-2772; order online at LifeWay.com; email
orderentry@lifeway.com; or visit the LifeWay Christian Store serving you.

Printed in the United States of America

Student Ministry Publishing
LifeWay Resources
One LifeWay Plaza
Nashville, TN 37234

# CONTENTS

# ABOUT *THE GOSPEL PROJECT*

*Gospel Foundations* is from the creators of *The Gospel Project*, which exists to point kids, students, and adults to the gospel of Jesus Christ through weekly group Bible studies and additional resources that show how God's plan of redemption unfolds throughout Scripture and still today, compelling them to join the mission of God.

The Gospel Project provides theological yet practical, age-appropriate Bible studies that immerse your entire church in the story of the gospel, helping to develop a gospel culture that leads to gospel mission:

## Gospel Story
Immersing people of all ages in the storyline of Scripture: God's plan to rescue and redeem His creation through His Son, Jesus Christ.

## Gospel Culture
Inspiring communities where the gospel saturates our experience and doubters become believers who become declarers of the gospel.

## Gospel Mission
Empowering believers to live on mission, declaring the good news of the gospel in word and deed.

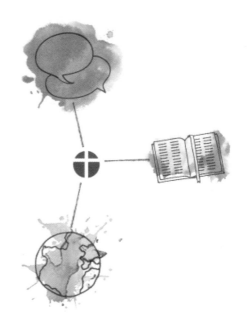

# HOW TO USE THIS STUDY

This Bible-study book includes seven weeks of content for group and personal study. Each session is divided into the following components:

## Introduction
Every session contains an intro option for your group time. allowing there to be a natural transition into the material for that week.

## Setting the Context
This section is designed to provide the context to the biblical passage being discussed. It will help group members to not only better understand the passage under consideration for each session, but also how the biblical storyline connects between each session. It is also in this section that you will find the reference to the informational graphic for each session, once again helping students to have a deeper understanding into the storyline of Scripture.

## Session Videos
Each session has a corresponding video to help tell the Bible story. After watching the video, spend some time discussing the questions provided, as well any additional questions raised by your students in response to the video.

## Group Discussion
After watching the video, continue the group discussion by reading the Scripture passages and discussing the questions on these pages. Additional content is also provided on these pages to grant additional clarity into the meaning of these passages. In addition, it is in this section that you find the Christ Connection, showing students how all of Scripture points to Jesus.

## Head, Heart, Hands
This section is designed to close out your group time by personally reflecting on how God's Story challenges the way we think, feel, and live as a result. Because God's Word is capable of changing everything about a person, this section seeks to spell out how each session is able to transform our Heads, Hearts, and Hands.

## Personal Study
Five personal devotions are provided for each session to take individuals deeper into Scripture and to supplement the content introduced in the group study. With biblical teaching and introspective questions, these sections challenge individuals to grow in their understanding of God's Word and to respond in faith.

# GOD'S WORD TO YOU

## *A SON WAS BORN FOR YOU*

Isaiah 9:6: "For a child will be born for us, a son will be given to us."

A Son will be given—a gift, a present. Isaiah lived in days shadowed by gloom, but God granted a flicker of hope, a ray of light—a Son would be given, a descendant of King David would come, an eternal kingdom would be established, one marked by justice and righteousness.

Yet God's people were shrouded in gloom for their lack of justice and righteousness. Their idolatry, their sin, brought God's judgment and their exile to the nations. They were meant to be a light to the nations; instead, they were nearly snuffed out. Still, a flicker of hope, a ray of light—a Child would be born. Through many dark days and years of God's silence, the flicker remained until the Son at last was given.

Matthew 1:21: "She will give birth to a son, and you are to name him Jesus, because he will save his people from their sins."

God presents His gift, the Son. And this Son answers the question, He solves the problem of their gloom—He will save His people from their sins. Their lack of justice and righteousness will be made up in His fullness. Their idolatry and sin will be done away with in His sacrifice. The flicker rages; the ray bursts forth; the Light has come to His people—and more.

Luke 2:10-11: "But the angel said to them, 'Don't be afraid, for look, I proclaim to you good news of great joy that will be for all the people: Today in the city of David a Savior was born for you, who is the Messiah, the Lord.' "

The present, the gift, is for all the people. The Savior from sins is for all the people; the Messiah-King is for all the people. Repent of your sin and believe in Jesus, who died for sins and rose from the dead that you may have life. "See, now is the acceptable time; now is the day of salvation!" (2 Cor. 6:2).

# THE BIRTH OF JESUS

*JESUS' BIRTH IS THE FULFILLMENT OF
GOD'S PROMISES.*

# INTRODUCTION

God left no doubt about what He expected from His people. As a jealous and loving God, He demanded holistic devotion that stemmed from the heart, not the halfhearted attempts of worship that were happening in the days of Malachi. The message of the Book of Malachi reminds us of our inability to love God because of our sin-tainted hearts, but we also hear the echoing promise of God to provide the coming Messiah, who would bring victory—true and lasting freedom—to His people.

▶ What do you think the four hundred years of silence between the Old and New Testaments was like for God's people?

The final words of the Old Testament are a curse, one that still hangs over sinful humanity. This curse cannot be lifted by our efforts. The only solution is a new heart rid of sin, and after four hundred years of silence, God provided the remedy for sin we need through the birth of a child, His Son, Jesus. The God whom humanity had sinned against would provide forgiveness of sin by taking on humanity Himself.

# SETTING THE CONTEXT

The four hundred years between the end of the Old Testament and the beginning of the New Testament is referred to as the intertestamental period and included a lot of political turmoil for the Jews, but the one true God was still present and unchanging.

The Persian Empire was conquered by Alexander the Great of Macedonia, who introduced Greek culture and the Greek language into the conquered territories of his empire. After Alexander's death, a series of successors ruled Judea. Then around 63 BC, the Roman Empire seized control. Two important religious and political groups emerged during this time. The Pharisees were committed to God's law, as supplemented by their own oral traditions. The Sadducees rejected most of the Old Testament and aligned themselves closely with Rome.

This was the climate in Judea when Jesus was born. In the fullness of time, in the fullness of Scripture, as "Hearing the Old Testament in Jesus' Birth" (p. 10) shows, God's Rescuer had come, not to free His people from Rome but from sin.

# HEARING THE OLD TESTAMENT
## IN JESUS' BIRTH

| OLD TESTAMENT | NEW TESTAMENT |
|---|---|
| **God Promised**<br>A Seed to Abraham<br>(Gen. 12; 15; 17) | **Jesus**<br>The Son of Abraham, the Seed<br>(Matt. 1:1; Gal. 3:16) |
| **God Promised**<br>A Descendant on David's Throne Forever<br>(2 Sam. 7) | **Jesus**<br>The Son of David, the Son of God<br>(Matt. 1:1; Luke 1:32) |
| **Immanuel**<br>A Sign Conceived by a Virgin<br>(Isa. 7:14) | **God Is with Us**<br>The Son Born to Mary, a Virgin<br>(Matt. 1:18-23) |
| **From Bethlehem**<br>Would Come God's Ruler over Israel<br>(Mic. 5:2) | **In Bethlehem**<br>The Messiah Was Born<br>(Matt. 2:1-6; Luke 2:1-6) |
| **A Star**<br>From Jacob, a Scepter from Israel<br>(Num. 24:17) | **The King of the Jews**<br>Heralded by a Star<br>(Matt. 2:1-2,9-10) |

# SESSION VIDEOS

Watch this session's video, and then continue the group discussion using the following guide.

▶ What ideas or phrases stood out to you most in the video? Why?

▶ The Book of Malachi left us wondering if the people of God would be ready for the Messiah. Were they? Why or why not?

# GROUP DISCUSSION

**As a group, read Luke 1:26-38.**

⭐ Why is it important to see Jesus as the fulfillment of God's promises in the Old Testament?

▶ What qualities of God's character are displayed in His choice of Mary?

It is not surprising to see that Luke, who was a doctor, was interested in the marginalized people of his day. After a brief introduction (vv. 1-4), Luke began the story of Jesus by telling of the miraculous promise of the birth of Jesus' cousin, John the Baptist. Miraculous promises were made to both sets of parents. Elizabeth and Zechariah, though well along in years, would have a son named John. Mary, who was twice described as a virgin, would give birth to Jesus. These were seemingly impossible promises, fulfilled through the poor and the marginalized.

God sent Gabriel to prepare Mary to be the mother of the Messiah. Mary was filled with both fear and awe in Gabriel's presence. The angel's message was troubling because of its supernatural nature, but at the same time it was filled with hope. Mary's Son would be great, He would be called "the Son of the Most High," and God would give Him the throne of David. The baby Mary would deliver would be the fulfillment of God's centuries-old promise of a king from David's family who would establish an eternal kingdom.

Mary responded with faith. She declared herself to be the servant of the Lord, her master. This was her identity. After all, servants have no choices; they surrender themselves to their masters. Even though there was much that Mary did not know, she had a deep-rooted faith and trust, and that is where her submissive spirit came from. She was ready to submit to God's difficult plan for her life.

# GROUP DISCUSSION *CONT.*

**As a group, read Luke 1:51-55.**

⭐ How was Jesus' birth related to God's promise to Abraham?

▶ What aspects of God's character and work did Mary highlight in her praise?

▶ What examples of these aspects of God have you seen in your life?

Mary's language revealed a heart and mind that must have been saturated with the Psalms. For the moment, she became a psalmist herself. And, like David she understood that the new hope being born into the world was based on an ancient hope.

The God of the Gospels is a God constantly turning the world upside down. The new hope that was born—the hope that is the subject of so many songs in the Scriptures—was granted to the outsiders, to the poor in spirit. In order to be rich, we learn to let go of our riches. In order to become wise, we embrace the foolishness of the cross. In order to become mature, we become like little children. In order to become truly free, we become slaves. Jesus wins everything by losing everything.

**As a group, read Luke 2:4-7.**

▶ Why are the circumstances of Jesus' birth so surprising?

⭐ What does the setting of Jesus' birth tell us about God's intent in sending Him?

Luke recounted the nativity of Jesus in four simple verses. Joseph made the trip from Galilee south to Judea and to Bethlehem, a city that lived in the shadow of one of Herod's fortresses. Mary, his pregnant fiancé, was with him because both of them would be included in the census.

Too often, the manger scenes and Christmas plays and sermons obscure the context of Jesus' birth. By reading the text and studying a little Jewish background, the reality of the conditions Jesus was born into become clear. Although "inn" is almost certainly a mistranslation, there indeed was no room in the guest room or lodging place, which would have been a part of any moderately-sized home. The point is not the nature of Jesus' birthplace but that there was no room—the Son of God was not even provided a proper place to be born! The only space left would have been the place where the animals were kept, which was usually a cave underneath the house.

▶ Based upon these passages, how does the biblical description of Jesus' birth differ from our modern day understanding?

## CHRIST CONNECTION

*The birth of Jesus fulfilled several Old Testament promises concerning the coming Messiah. Jesus was born in humble circumstances to be the Suffering Servant who would lay down His life as our mighty Savior. One day, Jesus will return as our eternal King.*

# OUR MISSION

## ◯ Head

How does Mary's response—calling herself the Lord's servant and willingly submitting to His will—reveal the posture every faithful Christian should have?

Name two or three of your favorite songs that magnify the Lord for His goodness and mercy. Why do these songs resonate with you? What aspects of God's character do they celebrate?

## ♥ Heart

How does Mary's faith as a young teenager encourage you in your own obedience to God?

If you were to compose your own song of thankfulness to God for His mercy in your life, what themes would you would touch on and why?

## ✋ Hands

In what ways has your relationship with Jesus changed your own life?

How can our willingness to share Christ with others serve as a sort of spiritual thermometer in our relationship with Him?

# PERSONAL STUDY: DAY 1

⭐ **The point: God sent John as Jesus' forerunner to help turn the hearts of God's people back to Him.**

▶ **Read Luke 1:5-25.**

What do these verses tell us about John?

v. 13: He was born to _____ and _____. His name was given by an _____.

v. 14: He would cause many to _____.

v. 15: He would be great in the _____ of the _____. He would be filled with the _____ _____.

v. 16: He would _____ many of the _____ to God.

v. 17: He would go before _____ in the spirit and power of Elijah. He would make the people ready for _____ _____.

God created John with a specific purpose in mind and had a plan for how He would use John to draw others to Himself.

Looking at verse 17, list the three specific things John would accomplish.

There was work to do before Jesus arrived, and John helped to prepare the way. Similarly, there is work for us to do before Jesus returns. How can you help prepare the way?

▶ **Respond**

Take a minute to think about the gifts and abilities God has given to you. Then answer these questions:

• How do your gifts and abilities play into God's ultimate goal of bringing others to know Him?
• In what ways can you use your life to glorify God?

# PERSONAL STUDY: DAY 2

⭐ **The point: Believers should submit to God's plans, even when they are difficult.**

▶ **Read Luke 1:26-38.**

When the angel appeared to Mary and told her what would happen to her, how did she react?

Mary asked the angel a question in verse 34, but her question was more about wanting to know the details rather than questioning God's plan. Despite her fears, Mary was submissive to God.

What did she call herself in verse 38? What does this tell us about her character? Explain.

The angel and his announcement may have startled Mary; however, Mary didn't let her fear keep her from stepping out in faith and accepting God's calling on her life. Mary held to the truth of God's Word.

Summarize the truth in verse 37.

▶ **Respond**

What are you struggling with? What has God called you to do that makes you afraid?

Mary called herself God's servant, even when what He asked her to do was difficult. List a few ways that you can serve God this week.

# PERSONAL STUDY: DAY 3

⭐ **The point: God's people trust Him to keep His promises.**

▶ **Read Luke 1:51-55.**

Mary experienced God's faithfulness and expressed her praise. Notice the verbs she used. Jot down what God did according to each verse.

v. 51

v. 52

v. 53

v. 54

v. 55

What does each of these actions say about God's character? (For example, in verse 51, we see God's strength.)

v. 51

v. 52

v. 53

v. 54

v. 55

What major promise did Mary mention God fulfilling in verses 54-55?

Each of the characteristics of God that Mary praised demonstrates the ways God keeps His promises. Mary understood that the child she carried was the promised Messiah the Israelites had longed, prayed, and waited for.

▶ **Respond**

Spend a couple of minutes in prayer, reflecting on this truth: If you're a follower of Christ, you are a part of God's people.

Record these three reminders: God is trustworthy, God is faithful, and God cares. Confess any doubts you have about God's faithfulness.

⭐ **The point: Jesus was born in humble circumstances.**

▶ **Read Luke 2:1-7.**

Indicate words in the text that emphasize the lowly nature of Jesus' birth.

As we recall the events surrounding the Jesus' birth, we understand the significance of this humble beginning. We understand that Jesus' birth in a manger was truly a significant and meek way for God's only Son, our Savior, to be welcomed into this world. Compare and contrast the way people viewed His birth then and what it means to us now.

Then

Now

How do you think it affects us to know the whole story—why Jesus was born into humble circumstances and why that's important?

Modern-day interpretations often obscure the context of Jesus' birth. How would you describe Jesus' birth according to the passages you read today?

▶ **Respond**

Jot down three words that come to mind when you think about Jesus' humble beginning.

Think about the way you respond when you hear the word humility. Then consider this: Jesus demonstrated true humility, not just by being born in a stable and wrapped in strips of cloth but also by becoming human and coming to Earth.

# PERSONAL STUDY: DAY 5

⭐ **The point: Jesus was born for the poor and the outcast.**

▶ **Read Luke 2:8-20.**

The angels could have gone to anyone first with the good news of Jesus' birth. Why do you think they chose the shepherds?

How did the shepherds respond to the angels' news? Why is this significant?

When the shepherds found everything just as the angels told them, what did they do?

Note the reaction others had to the shepherds' news.

▶ **Respond**

Despite being outcasts, the shepherds were the first people to hear about the birth of the Savior. Make a list of people or groups that you know who are often the marginalized in our society. Commit to praying for them this week.

Ask God to show you ways to share the good news with all people—regardless of their social status.

# THE PREPARATION
# OF JESUS

*JESUS OVERCAME TEMPTATION THROUGH THE
POWER OF GOD'S WORD.*

# INTRODUCTION

God's long promised rescue from sin and death was coming. But the rescue—and the Rescuer—had not burst onto the scene with great fanfare. Instead, Jesus was born in the most humble way imaginable: to a common family and in a stable. But this inauspicious birth was nevertheless the fulfillment of God's promises reaching back to the garden of Eden.

▶ How do the circumstances of Jesus' birth reflect His identity and mission in the world?

Looking back to the Old Testament, we see that the coming of Jesus was in no way haphazard or rushed. Instead, God had been preparing the world for the advent of His Son from the very beginning. Once born, God continued to prepare the way for His ministry and His message. Though Jesus was born in obscurity, He would soon step onto the public scene and change the world forever.

# SETTING THE CONTEXT

Mary and Joseph lived in Nazareth, but they were in Bethlehem when Jesus was born because of the Roman census. They stayed there for a time until an angel appeared to Joseph in a dream telling him to flee to Egypt to protect Jesus from King Herod, and they lived in Egypt until Herod died. Then they returned to Nazareth. These are the only details we know of Jesus' young childhood, but the Bible describes this time in simple but profound terms: "The boy grew up and became strong, filled with wisdom, and God's grace was on him" (Luke 2:40).

The only other glimpse into Jesus' boyhood involved one of the family's yearly trips to Jerusalem for Passover. When Jesus was twelve, He stayed behind in the temple while His parents started the journey back to Nazareth. When they realized He was not with them, they returned to Jerusalem and found Him in the temple, sitting with the teachers, amazing them with His questions and understanding of Scripture. And His explanation for His actions: "It was necessary for me to be in my Father's house" (2:49), reflecting the truth that "Jesus Is God" (p. 22). The rest of Jesus' growing up is summarized like this: "Jesus increased in wisdom and stature, and in favor with God and with people" (2:52).

# JESUS IS GOD

| PREEXISTENT | SON OF GOD | WORTHY OF WORSHIP | YAHWEH OF THE OLD TESTAMENT |
|---|---|---|---|
| • In the beginning, the Word was with God, and the Word was God; all of creation was made through Him—the Word became flesh (John 1:1-3,14) | • Conceived in Mary by the Holy Spirit, therefore called the Son of God (Matt. 1:18,20; Luke 1:35) | • *Quoting the Old Testament, Jesus Himself said worship should only be given to the Lord God* (Matt. 4:10) | • John the Baptist was God's messenger to prepare His way in the person of Jesus (Mark 1:2,4; Mal. 3:1) |
| • John the Baptist testified that the One who came after him—Jesus— existed before him (John 1:14-15) | • The fulfillment of the name "Immanuel," which means "God is with us" (Matt. 1:22-23) | • The wise men worshiped Jesus at His home in Bethlehem and gave Him gifts (Matt. 2:9-11) | • John the Baptist's mission was to "prepare the way for the Lord," who is Jesus (Mark 1:3-4; Isa. 40:3-5) |
| | • The voice from heaven proclaimed about Jesus at His baptism: "You are my beloved Son" (Mark 1:11) | • Jesus' disciples worshiped Him after He walked on the water and came to them in their boat (Matt. 14:33) | |
| | | • The women at Jesus' tomb worshiped Him after seeing His resurrection (Matt. 28:9) | |

# SESSION VIDEOS

Watch this session's video, and then continue the group discussion using the following guide.

▶ What ideas or phrases stood out to you most in the video? Why?

▶ What do we learn about battling temptation from Jesus' encounter with Satan in the wilderness?

# GROUP DISCUSSION

**As a group, read Mark 1:1-8.**

▶ How do you think John saw himself based on these verses? What can we learn from the way he viewed himself?

★ How would you explain repentance to a non-Christian?

God used John the Baptist as a spokesman—a prophet who would announce the arrival of Jesus and call on the people to prepare to meet their King through repentance. To repent means to turn away from sin and ourselves and toward God. This is a message we continue to preach. Like the people of Judea in John the Baptist's day, we too must prepare ourselves to meet Jesus by turning from sin and to Him.

**As a group, read Mark 1:9-11.**

★ Why was Jesus baptized even though He didn't need to repent of sin?

▶ What is so significant about the voice of God from heaven as Jesus was baptized?

▶ Why is baptism an important step for followers of Jesus today?

Jesus' baptism signaled the beginning of His public ministry. Jesus was not baptized for the forgiveness of sin—He committed no sin requiring such forgiveness—but to identify Himself and His ministry with the ministry and message of John the Baptist. When Jesus was baptized in the river that day, He also identified with sinners who repented and believed. Likewise, we associate ourselves with the people of God and share our commitment to Him when we are baptized. God was pleased with His Son for His obedience, and when we repent of sin and believe in Christ, God pronounces the same affirmation over us.

**As a group, read Matthew 4:1-11.**

▶ Why is it significant that the Spirit led Jesus into the wilderness to be tempted by the devil?

★ How was the temptation of Jesus similar to and different from the temptation Adam and Eve experienced in the garden?

Satan's intent was revealed in the opening words of his first assault: He questioned Jesus' identity as the Son of God. In order to understand the strategy Satan used against Jesus, we must understand how his opening move was intended to lead Jesus to doubt His identity and to indulge an earthly appetite.

Jesus fasted for forty days, so Satan attacked Him at His weakest moment. Behind the temptation to turn the stones into bread was the assumption that physical food is the most important nourishment we need, but Jesus' response said otherwise. In each of the three temptations, Jesus quoted from the book of Deuteronomy. His reference here, to Deuteronomy 8:3, stated the Word of God as the most vital nourishment.

Bread is one of the sustaining foods for physical life. However, more important than bread is the life of the Spirit. Our spiritual lives are sustained by the Word of God. Jesus understood that although His body was starving, He had feasted on God's Word, spoken over Him at the Jordan River. Jesus knew He was the Son of God—not a starving beggar in the wilderness, but a Son who delighted in the Word of His Father.

▶ In what way did the Word of God sustain Jesus when the Devil tempted Him? How did this relate to Jesus' identity?

Jesus' experience helps us understand our own struggle against temptation in our personal wilderness. God's Word provides the basis of our confidence. Our faith and trust in His Word provides the strength to resist Satan's continual lies. If Jesus had to rely on the Word of God, how much more should we?

Satan (the "accuser") always seeks to plant doubts in our minds—doubts that say God is not trustworthy. Jesus' life and obedience is a constant reminder that the Father can be trusted in every situation. Satan sows seeds of condemnation and confusion, but God's Word is rich in encouragement and clarity. Satan knows that if he can introduce the smallest doubt, he will have his foot in the door. But, if we continue in fellowship with God and walk with Jesus in the light of His Word, Satan is already defeated.

## CHRIST CONNECTION

*God declared that Adam was good, yet Adam failed to obey God, and the entire world experienced the consequences of his sin. Jesus is the Second Adam, and God declared Him pleasing because Jesus overcame temptation, refused to doubt, and lived a life of perfect obedience to the Father. Jesus' obedience and faithfulness to the Father is what led Him to the cross, the place where He conquered the sin brought on by Adam and showed He is the Savior of the world.*

# OUR MISSION

## O Head

When have you had a "wilderness" experience in your life spiritually? Did it seem like a test? Why or why not?

How does this account change the way you view difficult times in your life? What are some important lessons we can learn through times like these?

## ♥ Heart

Satan tried to manipulate the true meaning of God's Word in his attack on Jesus. What does this teach us about our need to properly understand God's Word?

Do you hunger for God's Word just as much as you hunger for food? Why or why not? What are some ways you can begin to increase your appetite for God's Word in your life?

## ✋ Hands

Why would it have been wrong for Jesus to turn the stones into bread? What does Jesus' answer teach us about the importance of God's Word?

How might you become equipped to use the power of God's Word in your own fight against sin? How equipped are you?

# PERSONAL STUDY: DAY 1

## ⭐ The point: The messenger's appearance pointed to Old Testament prophecy.

▶ **Read Mark 1:1-6.**

What did John do in order to prepare the way for the Lord?

Highlight the name of the prophet in the Book of Mark who predicted this messenger would come.

▶ **Read Isaiah 40:3.**

Both Mark and Isaiah mentioned that this messenger would carry out his ministry in the wilderness. What other time did God lead His people into the wilderness?

▶ **Read Malachi 3:1.**

Highlight the purpose of the messenger's coming. Why do you think it was necessary for the people to be prepared for the arrival of Christ?

John and Jesus both had a message. Compare and contrast the messages they spoke.

▶ **Respond**

God fulfilled prophecy in John's ministry and in Christ's coming. John prepared the way; Jesus was the way! In what ways does reading about God fulfilling His promises increase your faith?

In today's reading, the wilderness was symbolic of a movement of God. God led people to the wilderness and lives were changed. This was not the first time God had used the wilderness in such a way. Have you had any "wilderness" experiences? Consider that even there, God's promises never fail.

⭐ **The point: Jesus was tempted to gratify His desires apart from God's will.**

▶ **Read Matthew 4:1-4.**

Jesus knew His identity as God's Beloved Son. This was affirmed when the Spirit descended upon Him and God spoke at His baptism. What is significant about Satan's attack on Jesus' identity?

The Devil knew Jesus was hungry and tempted Him to satisfy His physical hunger. In response, Jesus quoted Deuteronomy 8:3. How did Jesus use this verse to show the importance of spiritual nourishment over physical appetite? What did this say about Jesus?

Jesus was tempted but did not succumb to temptation. List some words to describe how Jesus must have felt physically. Then describe the way He stood strong spiritually, despite His hunger.

| Physical Feelings | Spiritual Response |
| --- | --- |
| | |

▶ **Respond**

Jesus refused to give in to the temptation of physical hunger when He knew His need was spiritual. Take a minute to journal how Jesus' example motivates you to face temptation.

Although our bodies need food, God's Word sustains our spiritual lives. Formulate a plan to help you include a steady, daily diet of God's Word.

⭐ **The point: Jesus was tempted to test God and doubt His promises.**

▶ Read Matthew 4:5-7.

When Satan took Jesus to the temple in the Holy City, in what way did he tempt Jesus to test God?

How was the Devil's approach different from the other times he tempted Jesus?

Satan tested Jesus' trust and faith in God. However, Jesus refused and again used the Word of God as His defense. What did Jesus' response indicate about His trust and confidence in God? How does this give you confidence in God?

▶ **Respond**

Take some time to research and familiarize yourself with stories in the Bible where God proved Himself reliable and trustworthy. What advice would you give to a person who is struggling to have trust and confidence in God? Which Scriptures would you use to help him or her?

Ask yourself: Have I ever tested God, doing things that were risky as if to ask God to prove His love to me?

⭐ **The point: Jesus was tempted to exalt Himself apart from the cross.**

▶ **Read Matthew 4:8-10.**

Imagine the power and riches the kingdoms of the world displayed. How do you think this would be a temptation?

What did the Devil promise Jesus he would do for Him? What would Jesus have to do in order to receive what the Devil promised?

What did Jesus' response say about who He intended to worship? Why do you think He chose not to glorify Himself?

▶ **Respond**

Jesus chose to be obedient and humble, glorifying God instead of exalting Himself. We should also live for Him every day instead of living for ourselves. On a blank piece of paper, make two columns. In one column, list ways you intended to live for God, yet wound up living for yourself. In the other, list ways when you felt you lived for God despite the temptation to live for yourself.

Jesus knew four important things: He knew who He was, He knew the Father, He knew His Father's Word, and He knew God's plan. What does this tell us about ways we can stand strong when tempted to exalt ourselves?

# PERSONAL STUDY: DAY 5

⭐ **The point: Jesus overcame temptation and returned to Galilee.**

▶ **Read Matthew 4:11-16.**

What three things happened after Jesus told Satan to "Go away" (Matt. 4:10)?

Jesus was tempted but never gave in. What does Jesus' success over temptation say about the way He understands us? What does this tell you about His relationship with us?

By going to Galilee, Jesus fulfilled a prophecy from Isaiah. What was that prophecy?

Why is it important to note that Jesus fulfilled this prophecy?

▶ **Respond**

Jesus was tempted just like you are, overcame the temptation, and gives us the ability to resist temptation and continue to live on mission for Him.

List two practical ways you've learned to overcome temptation this week.

Thank God that you have a Savior who understands what it's like to be tempted, who perfectly resisted that temptation, and gave us an example of how to resist temptation too.

# THE MIRACLES
# OF JESUS

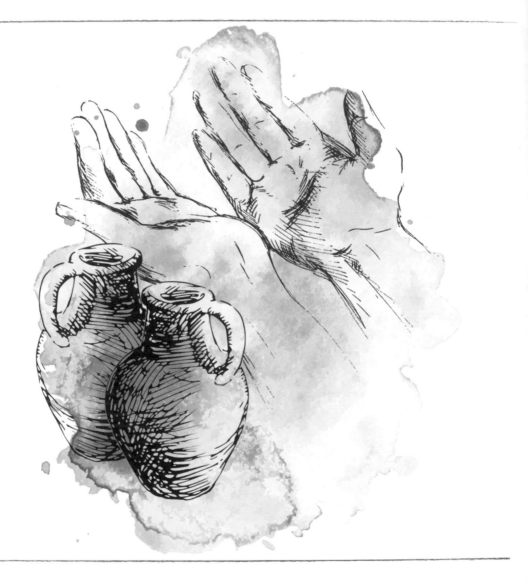

*JESUS' MIRACLES VERIFIED WHO HE IS.*

# INTRODUCTION

Jesus' public ministry began with an affirmation by His Father and an attack by Satan. The Son of God prevailed where all humanity had failed, but it would not be the last time Jesus squared off against the enemy. Jesus had maintained His trust in the Father and obeyed His will. This same trust and obedience would carry Jesus forward on His trajectory to the cross as the Savior of the world.

John had prepared Jesus' way, the Father had pronounced His approval, and now the Son had passed the test and would begin His public ministry. But as with His birth and baptism, Jesus' ministry would bring as much confusion and controversy as it did hope. As He began to travel, minister, and teach, Jesus embodied the mission and plan of God. He would, through His work and miracles, show us the nature of God's kingdom and reveal His own identity to those willing to see.

 What, in your understanding, was the purpose of Jesus' miracles?

# SETTING THE CONTEXT

John the Baptist, the forerunner of the Messiah, came upon hard days after the baptism of Jesus. He was arrested, imprisoned, and eventually beheaded by Herod.

Meanwhile, Jesus, having resisted the temptation of the enemy in the wilderness, began His public ministry in Galilee, the northernmost province in Palestine. Jesus would center most of His ministry there.

As Jesus traveled, His basic message was the two-pronged message of the gospel—repent and believe. He also spoke extensively on the kingdom of God and performed miracles among the people. The Jewish people had longed for this, but there was a great deal of misunderstanding about the identity and purpose of Jesus in fulfilling the kingdom of God. "Jesus' Signs in the Gospel of John" (p. 34) reveals the purpose and result of some of Jesus' miracles, along with some of the positive and negative responses.

# JESUS' SIGNS IN THE GOSPEL OF JOHN

| MIRACLE | PURPOSE | RESULT |
|---------|---------|--------|
| **FIRST SIGN:** Turning Water into Wine (John 2:1-12) | Revealed Jesus' glory as the Son of God | Revealed Jesus' glory as the Son of God |
| **SECOND SIGN:** Healing an Official's Son (John 4:46-54) | — | The royal official and his household believed in Jesus |
| **THIRD SIGN:** Healing a Man Disabled for 38 Years (John 5:1-18) | Demonstrated Jesus' unity with the Father and authority over the Sabbath | The Jews began persecuting Jesus |
| **FOURTH SIGN:** Feeding of 5,000 (John 6:1-15) | Demonstrated Jesus, the bread of life, was greater than Moses (John 6:32-35) | The crowd wanted to make Jesus king by force, but He withdrew from them |
| **FIFTH SIGN:** Walking on Water (John 6:16-21) | Demonstrated Jesus' identity as "I AM" | — |
| **SIXTH SIGN:** Healing a Man Born Blind (John 9) | Displayed God's works in the man's healing | The man believed in Jesus and worshiped Him |
| **SEVENTH SIGN:** Raising Lazarus from the Dead (John 11) | Displayed God's glory and glorified the Son of God | Many believed in Jesus, but the Sanhedrin plotted to kill Him |

# SESSION VIDEOS

**Watch this session's video, and then continue the group discussion using the following guide.**

▶ What ideas or phrases stood out to you most in the video? Why?

▶ Why is it important to note that the miracles of Jesus were intended to reveal His identity and character?

# GROUP DISCUSSION

**As a group, read Mark 1:21-28.**

▶    What does it mean to say that Jesus taught with authority?

★    Why were the miracles of Jesus essential to His authority?

Jesus demonstrated the authority of His words by the power of His works. Anyone could say whatever he or she wanted. But could anyone do what Jesus did?

While Jesus was teaching, He was interrupted by the cries of a man possessed by unclean spirits. But these were not wordless exclamations; in fact, the question the man asked reveals that demons knew more about this new teacher than the people listening to Him. And these demons knew that the authority and mission of Jesus would bring judgment. He didn't need to appeal to a greater power or use some authoritative incantation to cast out the demons; He simply uttered a command. He was the ultimate authority, and He exercised that authority over the spirits. Once again, the people were amazed. They had never experienced anything like this—a teacher who not only taught with authority but who backed up His teaching with authoritative action.

This same Jesus who spoke and acted in power and authority is the One we worship today. Just as He had authority in word and deed then, He holds the same power over us and our circumstances today. But like the people in Capernaum, we must not only marvel at the power of Jesus—we must recognize His authority and submit our lives to it.

**As a group, read Mark 1:35-38.**

▶    What does this practice of Jesus teach us about the nature and necessity of prayer?

▶    How did the disciples' priorities differ from Jesus' in this scene?

★    What can we learn about how Jesus viewed His mission from these verses?

# GROUP DISCUSSION *CONT.*

Jesus' authority, as displayed in both His teaching and His miraculous power, certainly generated great discussion among the people, and His fame spread like a brush fire in a dry climate. Word of this upstart rabbi swept through the communities of Palestine. The whole town of Capernaum showed up for an audience with Jesus after they heard of His teaching and miracles. By the end of the day, Jesus had healed many people of their diseases and cast out demons. It had been a full day to say the least.

The next morning, Jesus went off alone to pray. The Son of God consistently made time to pray during His earthly ministry. Jesus would set aside everyone and everything to be with the Father (Mark 6:46; 14:32-41). Most of us should feel crushing conviction of how little we prioritize prayer in comparison.

But why did Jesus pray? He prayed because He knew that this was just the beginning. The crowds would grow. The pressure would mount. The temptation to veer from the will of God would increase. To continue in His ministry and stay focused on the mission and will of the Father, He needed these times of prayer. But His disciples had other ideas.

### As a group, read Mark 1:39-42.

▶  How did the leper in this passage express faith?

★  Why is it significant that Jesus was moved to compassion and reached out and touched the man?

With Jesus' response we see an unthinkable act of One driven by compassion. This man was not an obstacle to His mission to preach the good news of the kingdom. The compassion He felt for this man was a hallmark of that very kingdom, rooted in God's self-determined compassion for sinful humanity that led to Jesus' arrival in the first place. Rather than ignoring the man or turning away from him in disgust, rather than rebuking the man for not following the law or interrupting Him, Jesus reached out to the man and touched him.

Notice that Jesus didn't heal the man's skin disease first and then touch him. The Son of God bent low and placed His hands on the man's diseased body. Perhaps this was the first touch the leper had felt for months or even years. And in touching him, Jesus violated the ceremonial law that kept the man at a distance from other people. But in His touch, Jesus revealed that in the kingdom, love and compassion rule over ritual and regulation.

Praise the Lord it is so—not only for the leper, but for us as well. Jesus did not keep us, in our sinful uncleanness, at an arm's length. No, He bent low to us, so low that He came from heaven and was born as a servant, immersing Himself in sinful humanity (while Himself remaining sinless).

## CHRIST CONNECTION

*From the very beginning of Jesus' early ministry, the people recognized that He was different, largely because of the power and authority He demonstrated through His miracles. Jesus' miracles proved He is the Son of God and also revealed His love and compassion for the people He came to save.*

# OUR MISSION

 **Head**

Can you relate to the leper? When is a time that you have felt unclean and yet sensed the touch of Jesus?

What is the danger in seeking Jesus because of what we think He might be able to do for us?

 **Heart**

What are some ways we as Christians fall short of living under Jesus' authority and can merely be impressed with His teaching?

Is there anything causing you to question either the power or authority of Jesus? What is God calling you to do instead?

**Hands**

Is there any group of people that you would deem too unclean for you to be around? What are the implications of Jesus' interaction for how you see those people?

How should we understand the place of Jesus' miracles given His focus on mission?

# PERSONAL STUDY: DAY 1

★ **The point: Our faith is a desperate pursuit of restoration with God, fulfilled through Jesus Christ.**

▶ Read Mark 2:1-4.

Jesus had just returned from preaching and performing miracles in other cities and word spread quickly. Why do you think so many people gathered in His home?

Although Jesus was probably exhausted from His journey, He was ready and willing to speak to the crowd. What does this reveal about His character?

Why do you think the paralyzed man's friends were so determined to bring their friend to Jesus? What actions revealed their determination?

In order to accomplish their goal, these men had to sacrifice their convenience. What are you willing to sacrifice for your friends to be introduced to Jesus' healing power?

▶ Respond

Think of a friend or family member who needs to know God's forgiveness and healing. Ask God to give you opportunities to share with them how they can find forgiveness through Jesus.

# PERSONAL STUDY: DAY 2

⭐ **The point: The area in which we need the most healing isn't physical but spiritual.**

▶ **Read Mark 2:5,9.**

Look back at verse 4. What initially kept the four friends from bringing the paralytic to Jesus?

What strikes you about Jesus' response to the paralyzed man and his friends?

Why do you think Jesus forgave the man's sins before He told him to pick up his mat and walk (v. 9)? What does this reveal about God's view of sin?

Notice how Jesus called the paralytic "son." What does this tell you about Jesus' relationship with those who have been forgiven?

It is much more important for someone to experience spiritual restoration rather than just physical healing. Read 2 Corinthians 5:20 and fill in the blanks:

We are _____ for Christ, and He _____ to the world through

us. We ask others to be _____ to God.

▶ **Respond**

What are some areas in your life where you still need healing? List them on a sticky note and remember to ask God for healing in each of these areas throughout the week.

Consider this: How am I acting as an ambassador for Christ? Who am I pleading with to be reconciled to God?

# PERSONAL STUDY: DAY 3

⭐ **The point: Jesus' claim that He could forgive sins placed Him as equal with God.**

▶ **Read Mark 2:6-7.**

Skim through Leviticus 24:15-16 in your Bible. What happened to people who blasphemed against God? How does this change your perspective on the scribes' question?

Who alone has the ability to forgive sins? Why is this important?

Review the thoughts of the scribes in verses 6-7. What does their reaction indicate about the importance of Jesus' statement (v. 5)?

How do we view Jesus' statement differently than the scribes would have? Explain.

▶ **Respond**

Have you ever heard someone say something about God that was disrespectful? How did you respond?

Spend a few minutes in prayer, asking God to help you discern the difference between truth and lies and to have the courage to call out blasphemy in truth and love.

# PERSONAL STUDY: DAY 4

⭐ **The point: Jesus provides relief for eternity.**

▶ **Read Mark 2:8-10.**

*Omniscience* is defined as *the ability to know all things*. How did Jesus demonstrate His omniscience in these verses?

What did Jesus mean when He asked if it was easier to forgive a man's sins or to tell him to get up and walk? Rewrite Jesus' statement in your own words.

What did Jesus say was His reason for performing this miracle (v. 10)? Why was this important for the scribes to understand? Why is it important for us to understand that Jesus has authority on earth?

▶ **Respond**

Think about your own life. Do you believe that Jesus has the authority to forgive sins?

Grab a colorful pen and some note cards. Look up the following verses about forgiveness, and write out each one on a separate card: Ephesians 4:32; Colossians 3:13; and 1 John 1:9. Post the cards where you will see them or carry them with you and look at them during quiet moments throughout the day as you remember God's grace toward you.

# PERSONAL STUDY: DAY 5

⭐ **The point: Jesus provides relief for our current situation.**

▶ **Read Mark 2:10-12.**

Describe this scene in your own words. How do you think everyone reacted as they saw the man get up?

Verse 12 says the man "immediately" got up from the mat and began walking around as if he was never paralyzed (v. 12). What does this tell you about Jesus' ability to heal?

Jesus performed this miracle not only for the scribes to see but also for the other people in the room. What was the ultimate result of Jesus' demonstration (v. 12b)?

List some situations today that people might see and then glorify God.

▶ **Respond**

List a few situations in your life in where you want to ask Jesus to provide relief or healing.

Consider this: Would I be able to live with these situations regardless of the outcome, knowing that I have received forgiveness and eternal hope from Jesus?

For further study of Jesus' healing, read Mark 5.

# THE TEACHINGS OF JESUS

*GOD'S GRACE IS OFFERED TO THOSE WHO REPENT OF THEIR SIN AND SELF-RIGHTEOUSNESS.*

# INTRODUCTION

Have you ever noticed how many children's films are about a character being separated from its father?

• *An American Tail* relates the story of Fievel, a mouse whose curiosity leads him to a forbidden part of a ship full of immigrants. In a terrible storm, Fievel is swept out to sea and spends the rest of the film trying to find his papa.

• *Finding Nemo* is about a little clown fish who rebels against his father's wishes, gets caught by a diver in the ocean, and ends up in an aquarium in a dentist's office. The film shows Nemo's dad, Marlin, traveling the ocean past sharks and jellyfish in order to find his son.

• *Annie* is about an orphan girl longing to be reunited with her parents.

• *Home Alone* tells the story of a boy who wishes his family was gone and comes to regret that wish!

Stories of separation and reunion, longing and fulfillment, exile and return strike a chord in our hearts. Why? Because these stories all somehow mirror the great story of the world, in which sinners who are lost and in bondage need to be found and set free.

# SETTING THE CONTEXT

Jesus taught with authority backed up by miracles, but what was the substance of that teaching? While Jesus taught on a variety of subjects, several themes were repeated in His teaching as He traveled throughout Palestine.

One unique characteristic of His stories was His use of unexpected heroes. Instead of positioning religious Jewish men at the center of His stories, Jesus often held up Gentiles, women, or even children as having characteristics that should be emulated.

One of the more distinct components of Jesus' teaching was His use of parables, a common form of teaching in Judaism to communicate rich meaning through memorable symbolism. Jesus, however, said that He taught in parables not because they were easy to remember but because teaching in parables actually separated those who were His disciples from those who weren't. "Parables of the Kingdom" (p. 46) recounts the kingdom significance of some of Jesus' parables.

# PARABLES *OF THE* **KINGDOM**

| | |
|---|---|
| **The Sower and the Soils** (Matt. 13:1-9,18-23; Mark 4:1-9, 13-20; Luke 8:4-8,11-15) | The word about the kingdom—the gospel—is fruitful only in a heart that hears and understands the good news, yet the message must still be shared like the indiscriminate casting of seed on the ground. |
| **The Hidden Treasure and the Priceless Pearl** (Matt. 13:44-46) | The kingdom is of such value that it is worth sacrificing everything we have in order to be a part of it. |
| **The Wicked Tenants** (Matt. 21:33-46; Mark 12:1-12; Luke 20:9-19) | The kingdom is comprised of people who produce its fruit; failure to produce fruit for God, exemplified in the rejection of His Son, Jesus, is to reject participation in the kingdom of God. |
| **The Good Samaritan** (Luke 10:25-37) | The kingdom is comprised of those who see themselves as neighbors without boundaries and who show mercy to others. |
| **The Lost Sheep/Coin/Sons** (Luke 15:1-32) | The kingdom of heaven rejoices over a sinner who repents; refusal to rejoice over a sinner's repentance is to find oneself on the outside of the kingdom. |
| **The Pharisee and the Tax Collector** (Luke 18:9-14) | The kingdom is comprised of those who humble themselves before God and rely solely upon God's mercy for their salvation; these will be exalted, but those who exalt themselves will be humbled. |

# SESSION VIDEOS

Watch this session's video, and then continue the group discussion using the following guide.

▶ What ideas or phrases stood out to you most in the video? Why?

▶ With whom do you identify in Jesus' story of the prodigal sons—the older or younger son? Why?

# GROUP DISCUSSION

**As a group, read Luke 15:11-13.**

▶ Why was the son's request so shocking?

⭐ What does the son's request reveal about our sin? What does the father's response reveal about the character of God?

In Jesus' day, it was normal for sons to assume that upon their father's death they would gain a sizeable inheritance, consisting of the family's assets and property. But in Jesus' parable, the younger son demanded his portion early. Today's equivalent would be a teenager spitting in his dad's face and screaming, "I want you dead!" Asking for the inheritance early suggested that the son couldn't wait for his father to die. He wanted what his father could give him now, even at the expense of their relationship.

A bigger shock followed—the father gave the younger son what he asked for. In fact, he gave both his sons their inheritance (v. 12). In those days, the older son would be expected to build a bridge between the father and the younger son and avoid public humiliation. But instead of trying to restore the family's fellowship, the older son silently took his double portion of the fortune. There was neither outcry against the younger brother's action nor passionate defense of the father's honor. The older son pocketed his inheritance, stayed home, and stayed quiet. His silence was deafening.

Jesus painted a picture of two types of lost people. The first is openly rebellious— the "in your face" sin of the younger son. The younger son's request illustrates the enormity and consequence of human sin. "God, we want what You can give us, but we don't want You!" The second is a more subtle type of sinner—seen in the older son. He represents someone who appears to be near God but is actually far away. He's the church member who wants God's blessing but could care less about God's name being honored or about glorifying God with his life. He doesn't care about his father or his brother—only about himself and what he can get out of the situation.

**As a group, read Luke 15:17-24.**

▶ When was a time in your life that you found yourself in a similar situation as the younger son?

▶ What are some of the ways the father might have responded to his son coming home?

⭐ Where do you see the gospel in his response?

Jesus' dramatic parable continues with the younger son converting his newly obtained property into cash. When the disgraceful deed was done, the prodigal son headed off to a far country, where he squandered all his wealth in reckless living. The boy wasted his money and life, so when the famine came, he wound up desperate. Not only did the younger son start working for a Gentile (bad enough in Jewish culture at the time), he was also actually feeding pigs—the most despised and unclean of animals for a Jew! The Jews in Jesus' audience must have bristled at such a terrible picture of this younger son's sin.

The crucial moment in Jesus' story occurred as the son approached his hometown. Jesus said that the father saw his son while he was still a long way off. This implies that the boy was probably at the edge of town, ready to head down the main street (which was usually the road that almost everyone in the village lived on). The father had been watching diligently, hoping to catch a glimpse of his son.

▶ Make a list of several characteristics communicated by the father's actions in this parable. How are these characteristics also true of God?

**As a group, read Luke 15:25-32.**

▶ Why is the older son angry? Does his anger surprise you? Why or why not?

⭐ What does this interaction with his father reveal about how the older son sees himself?

Finally, Jesus turned the focus back to the older son, who had not been mentioned since the beginning of the parable. We've seen the way the father ran to his ragged, prodigal son at the edge of the community. Similarly, the father went out to convince his puffed up and arrogant older son to come in and celebrate his brother's return. The loving father had two sons who blocked his love in different ways. The younger one had walled himself off from the father's love by doing evil, while the older one walled himself off from that same love by doing good. The older brother went through the motions so he could gain rights in the household, not true membership in the family. The younger brother—the repentant rebel—was inside feasting while the older brother—the "good" son—stayed outside pouting.

The older son refused to call the younger son his "brother." Instead, he only referred to him as his father's other son. Then Jesus ended His parable with the gracious father's response to his older son's complaint. Although the older son had lashed out and refused to address his dad respectfully, the father replied by calling him "son." The father reminded him of their shared relationship. He earnestly wanted his older son to come inside so that the family would be whole.

## CHRIST CONNECTION

*The Pharisees and scribes criticized Jesus for His practice of welcoming and dining with sinners. The stories Jesus told in response to their criticism focused on God's joy over sinners coming to repentance and illustrated His mission on earth. The God who seeks and saves the lost is Jesus, the Savior whose search and rescue mission is accomplished at great personal cost to Himself.*

# OUR MISSION

## Head

In what ways does the father's treatment of his son go above and beyond what anyone expected?

What are some specific ways this story pictures our salvation?

## Heart

Why does a heart closed off to God lead to a refusal to accept repentant sinners?

How does the gospel challenge and transform the closed-off heart?

## Hands

What are some common examples today of ways we might waste God's good gifts?

In what ways does wasting God's gifts lead to slavery instead of freedom?

# PERSONAL STUDY: DAY 1

## ✪ The point: We have all sinned and rebelled against God.

▶ **Read Luke 15:11-19.**

Religious leaders criticized and confronted Jesus for interacting with notorious sinners. This parable served to illustrate God's forgiveness to all kinds of sinners.

List the people mentioned in this passage.

What character traits did the younger son demonstrate when he demanded his inheritance?

What character traits did he reflect when he decided to return home?

How does the younger son's rebellion against his father reflect our rebellion against God?

▶ **Respond**

Think of some ways you, like the younger son, may communicate that you want God's blessings more than you want His glory. Commit to seeking God's will above all else.

Rebellion is the moment we choose sin. Repentance is the moment when we humble ourselves and come back to God. Confess any rebellion you have had in your heart and thank God for His forgiveness.

⭐ **The point: God celebrates when sinners turn toward Him in repentance.**

▶ **Read Luke 15:20-24.**

Highlight the words "a long way off." Jesus intentionally mentioned the son's distance from the father. The father had been watching and waiting for his son's return. In the same way, God longs for us to return to Him.

List out the actions of both the son and the father in this passage.

| Son's Actions | Father's Actions |
|---|---|
|  |  |

Look back over your list. What characteristics of God do you think Jesus was illustrating by the father's actions?

Summarize what the son said to his father. How does this relate to sinners today?

Not only did the father rejoice when the son first arrived, but he threw a celebration in honor of his son. How do you think this models God's reaction to those who place their faith in Jesus for salvation? (Hint: see at Luke 15:7.)

▶ **Respond**

Sometimes we don't confess our sin to God because we are embarrassed or ashamed. Jesus made it clear that God is pleased when we return to Him.

Spend a few minutes reflecting on your relationship with God and any sin that might be unconfessed.

## ⭐ The point: Some people resent God's grace and cling to religious observance.

Forgiveness is a gift from God that all believers have received. All offenses were wiped out on the cross for those who trust in Jesus as Savior.

▶ **Read Luke 15:25-32.**

What was the older brother's reaction to his brother's return?

How did the father respond to the older brother's refusal to celebrate?

Why did the brother claim to be justified in this response?

The father responded to his oldest son graciously, turning his attention away from the possessions, works, and obedience to their relationship and his relationship to the younger brother.

What are some similarities between the older brother and believers today?

▶ **Respond**

List some ways your focus is rerouted to works you've done rather than the grace God has given to you. Then, list some practical ways you can refocus on God's grace to you.

God calls all people in every part of the world to repentance, no matter how you feel or what you think about them. Jot down the names of two people or people groups you struggle to reach out to. Then, pray that God would soften your heart toward them and give you the courage to reach out to them.

## ⭐ The point: Repentance is shown through a transformed life and lasting change.

▶ **Read Psalm 119:57-60.**

The psalmist was moved to obedience because of the grace of God. The psalmist was grateful for his "portion"—the inheritance God promised to His people. So, with a grateful heart, the psalmist committed to actively pursuing God and keeping His words.

In what ways do the psalmist's words and actions point to a life transformed by God?

Highlight the actions the psalmist took as he pursued God. Then, explain in your own words which of those actions is the most difficult for you and why.

What are some obstacles all believers might face to true, lasting change?

▶ **Read Matthew 3:8.**

The word "produce" is incredibly active, as was the psalmist's pursuit of God. What does this tell you about living a life that is completely changed by the gospel?

▶ **Respond**

How is your life different because you know Jesus? Jot down some aspects of your life that you know are present only because you are joined with Christ.

How do you think others would characterize you? Would they see the fruit of repentance in your daily life?

# PERSONAL STUDY: DAY 5

⭐ **The point: Jesus' mission to restore the lost to a relationship with the Father cost Him His life.**

Indicate the synonym that you identify with the most when you feel helpless:

Defenseless     Vulnerable     Overcome     Weak

Abandoned     Powerless     Incapable     Useless

Use the word you chose to describe your relationship to sin before coming to know Jesus. For example, I was _____ against the power of sin and death.

▶ **Read Romans 5:6.**

Highlight the word "helpless." Sinners were helpless to defend against the temptation of sin and helpless to reconcile themselves with God because of the offense of our sin.

What other word is used in this verse to describe sinners?

How do these two words show the miracle of salvation?

▶ **Read 1 Corinthians 6:19-20.**

What does it mean that you were bought with a price? Explain.

What does it mean to say that you are not your own?

▶ **Respond**

Sin that involves our body can have serious consequences both physically and spiritually. What are some of the temptations that cause us to not honor God with our bodies?

SESSION 5

# THE CRUCIFIXION
# OF JESUS

*JESUS IS THE GOOD SHEPHERD WHO LAYS DOWN
HIS LIFE FOR HIS SHEEP.*

# INTRODUCTION

Jesus did not come to call the righteous but sinners. He did not come to heal the healthy but the broken. He did not come to lift up the proud but the humble. Through His ministry, Jesus welcomed those who recognized their need for salvation and who embraced the good news of the kingdom. In word and deed, Jesus showed that the gospel is for all, for all are sinners and all are in need of God's grace.

▶ What was your biggest insight through your study of Jesus' parable of the prodigal sons?

During His three-year ministry, Jesus taught thousands of people, performed numerous miracles, and turned Galilee, Judea, and Samaria upside down. But as impressive as these things were, they are all part of a bigger story—the story of redemption that was driving Jesus to the cross. At the cross, Jesus fulfilled His mission and, in so doing, satisfied the justice of God. It was at the cross where Jesus offered Himself as the punishment for sin and provided the way for humanity to be saved.

▶ What thoughts and feelings are raised when you think about Jesus' crucifixion?

# SETTING THE CONTEXT

The cross was never far from the mind of Christ. Throughout His teaching ministry, Jesus alluded to His death several times when speaking to His disciples. But His disciples failed to understand what Jesus was telling them.

After three years of ministry, Jesus approached Jerusalem knowing that He would hang on a cross within the week. Accordingly, He made final preparations for what would happen, including fulfilling the Old Testament prophecies of His entrance into Jerusalem, teaching in parables about the end of the age, and preparing for and eating the Passover meal with His disciples.

Meanwhile, the religious establishment made their preparations, also according to Scripture, to kill this threat to their power, including paying Judas, one of Jesus' disciples, to betray Him. "Jesus' Suffering" (p. 58) recounts the ways Jesus suffered as the climax of His life and ministry, according to the Father's plan.

# JESUS' *SUFFERING*

| JESUS' SUFFERING | OLD TESTAMENT TYPES AND PROPHECIES | JESUS' FOLLOWERS WILL SUFFER |
|---|---|---|
| **Jesus Was Betrayed** (Matt. 26:14-16, 47-50; John 13:18-27; Acts 1:16) | • A friend betrays (Ps. 41:9)<br>• 30 pieces of silver as a price (Zech. 11:12-13) | Betrayal by family and friends as those who hate Christ (Luke 21:16-17) |
| **Jesus Felt the Weight of the Cup of God's Wrath** (Matt. 26:36-44) | • The cup of the Lord's wrath (Isa. 51:17-20)<br>• The cup of wrath for the nations (Jer. 25:15-29) | **There is no condemnation for those who are in Christ Jesus (Rom. 8:1)** |
| **Jesus Was Mocked, Beaten, and Falsely Accused** (Matt. 26:57-68; 27:27-31,39-44) | • The Suffering Servant was despised and rejected, oppressed and afflicted (Isa. 53:3,7)<br>• The psalmist was scorned, despised, and mocked (Ps. 22:6-8) | Suffering and persecution at the hands of the world on account of Jesus' name (Matt. 5:10-11; John 15:20-21; 16:33) |
| **Jesus Was Crucified and Drank the Cup of God's Wrath in Our Place** (Matt. 27:33-50; John 19:16-37) | • The Passover (Ex. 11–13), reinstituted in the Lord's Supper—the bread (Jesus' broken body) and the cup of the new covenant (Jesus' shed blood)<br>• The psalmist felt abandoned by God (Ps. 22:1)<br>• The Suffering Servant pierced for others' rebellion (Isa. 53:5)<br>• It pleased the Lord to crush the Servant as an offering of atonement (Isa. 53:10) | **God made Him who had no sin to be sin for us so we might become the righteousness of God in Him (2 Cor. 5:21)** |

# SESSION VIDEOS

**Watch this session's video, and then continue the group discussion using the following guide.**

▶ What ideas or phrases stood out to you most in the video? Why?

▶ What are some ways we can combat an over-familiarity and coldness to the story of the cross?

# GROUP DISCUSSION

**As a group, read Mark 14:22-26.**

⭐ How did Jesus give new meaning to the Passover celebration?

▶ As the disciples observed and listened to Jesus at the first Lord's Supper, what do you think might have been going through their minds?

For more than a thousand years, God's people celebrated the Passover meal to remember the exodus, God's deliverance of His people from bondage in Egypt. But on the night of His betrayal, Jesus added new meaning to this meal. The Passover would no longer only look back at God's deliverance from Egyptian bondage through Moses, but it would also picture God's deliverance from sin's bondage through Christ.

Jeremiah and Ezekiel both prophesied about a day when hearts of stone would be replaced with hearts of flesh—when God's people would be cleansed of their sin, filled with God's Spirit, and be His people (Jer. 31:31-34; Ezek. 11:19-20; 36:26-36).

This new covenant, this new, one-time sacrifice, was what Jesus had in mind when He spoke of His body being broken and blood poured out during the Last Supper. What the disciples would see on the cross soon after would be the fulfillment of God's promises. No longer would God's people offer goats and bulls for their sin. God was offering Himself.

# GROUP DISCUSSION *CONT.*

Then Jesus offered what might have seemed to be an offhand remark, but it was actually a beautiful promise. It was a promise to give His disciples in the room that evening—and us—hope. Jesus would drink the fruit of the vine with them again. It would not be soon, but it would happen, and when it did, they would all be in His Father's kingdom.

### As a group, read Mark 14:32-36.

⭐ How does this garden scene compare with the first garden scene in the Bible—the garden of Eden? What temptations were presented in both?

▶ What was the focus of Jesus' prayers?

Jesus wanted to obey the Father. He wanted to bring the Father glory and be the One to bring salvation to the world. And yet, He knew what a Roman crucifixion was like. He understood that the physical agony He would feel would not be His greatest suffering—bearing the sins of the world and being separated from the Father would be. And so, He wrestled with what lay before Him. He was so distressed that He told His disciples He was "deeply grieved to the point of death."

But in the end, unlike Adam, Jesus submitted to the Father's will with an emphatic "not what I will, but what you will" (v. 36). Jesus knew that there was no way to fulfill the Father's Word other than by submitting to the Father's will. God would only take this cup away from His people by pouring it out on His righteous Servant (Isa. 51:17,21-22). Jesus received the wounds we deserved, and by faith we receive forgiveness we do not deserve (53:1-12).

This means that like Jesus, we are to submit to the Father's will, even when it results in suffering. We are called to follow Christ, which means we are called to suffer (1 Pet. 2:21). We should not be surprised when suffering comes our way; it is one way God transforms us into the image of His Son. The good news is, though, that by His death and resurrection, Jesus has granted us the power to face any and all suffering we may face (vv. 24-25).

### As a group, read Mark 15:22-41.

▶ Where do you see Psalm 69:21, Psalm 22:18, and Isaiah 53:12 fulfilled in Mark's account of the crucifixion?

Why is it significant that the curtain was ripped from top to bottom?

Jesus' cry should have resonated in the minds of the onlookers, but they missed His reference. These are the opening words of Psalm 22, a psalm dripping with messianic meaning (see especially vv. 1-2,6-8,12-18). Jesus was not calling upon Elijah, as the crowd supposed. He was identifying Himself as the One to whom the psalm pointed and demonstrating the horror of feeling forsaken by His Father.

And then Jesus let out His last breath. With it, the veil in the temple that separated heaven and earth was split from top to bottom, signifying that this act was accomplished from above.

In the torn curtain, a message is proclaimed. A Son was rejected so that the Father would have many more sons and daughters. The Father forsook His only Son that He might extend forgiveness to a great many children. A Son's sacrifice was accepted in the holy of holies that all who trust in Him might be accepted before the very throne of God.

## CHRIST CONNECTION

*Unjustly condemned to death, Jesus willingly took up His cross and suffered the judgment our sins deserve. At the moment He died, the curtain in the temple sanctuary was torn in two, signifying the truth that sinners have access to God through the blood of Christ. The crucifixion of Jesus is the center of history, revealing God's holiness and justice, our sinfulness and unrighteousness, and Christ's humility and love.*

# OUR MISSION

 **Head**

Why are people prone to miss Jesus' glory on the cross?

Have you ever submitted to the Father's will knowing it would bring suffering? How does understanding the purposes of God help you face suffering?

 **Heart**

What would it look like for a Christian to yearn for the consummation of the kingdom?

What excites you most about eternity future in God's kingdom?

 **Hands**

If a non-Christian asked you the question, "Why did Jesus die?" how would you respond?

How does meditating on Christ help you prepare for suffering? What does a Christ-like response to suffering look like?

# PERSONAL STUDY: DAY 1

⭐ **The point: At the Lord's Supper, Jesus talked about the sacrifice required by the new covenant.**

**Review John 13:1-15 for context.**

Summarize what happened before Jesus and the disciples participated in the first Lord's Supper.

▶ **Read Matthew 26:26-28.**

Describe what each element (the bread and the cup) represents.

| Bread | Cup |
|---|---|
| | |

What significance did eating the bread and drinking the cup have for the disciples? What significance does the Lord's Supper also have for us? Explain.

Jesus said His blood was poured out for the _____ of our _____.

▶ **Respond**

Think about what Jesus said. His body was broken for you. His blood was poured out for you. How will this change your attitude and perspective the next time you participate in the Lord's Supper?

For further study on the Lord's Supper, read 1 Corinthians 11:17-26.

⭐ **The point: Jesus revealed to His disciples that they would be in His Father's kingdom together.**

▶ **Read Matthew 26:29-30.**

What did Jesus say would be different "until that day"?

Jesus said He would see them again in His _____ _____.
Why was that such an encouragement for the disciples? Why is it such an encouragement to us?

What did they do after sharing the Lord's Supper? How does this help us understand the attitude we are to have when taking the Lord's Supper?

When you take the Lord's Supper, how does it help you remember the sacrifice Jesus made? Explain.

▶ **Respond**

Worship happens through participating in the Lord's Supper and singing praises together. Jesus revealed that He and His disciples would share this same kind of unity in God's future kingdom.

For further study on Jesus' followers' place in God's kingdom, read John 14:1-4.

⭐ **The point: The Lord's Supper is an act of obedience that believers participate in together.**

What kinds of images come to mind when you hear the word *obedience*?

▶ **Read 1 Corinthians 11:17-22.**

Why did Paul criticize the Corinthian church?

Highlight the word "divisions" in verse 18. Think about your own church and describe what you think Paul was talking about.

Why might divisions harm the church body or participation in the Lord's Supper?

How were the Corinthians misusing the Lord's Supper?

▶ **Respond**

Are you ever tempted to speak negatively about or dislike someone at church? Ask God to forgive your divisive spirit, even if you never intended to hurt God's church.

Ask the Holy Spirit to guide you as you examine your heart. Are there things for which you need to ask God's forgiveness?

Take a minute to confess those things to God. Then, ask Him to help you create unity rather than divisiveness among your Christian brothers and sisters.

SESSION 5.5

65

## ⭐ The point: Jesus agreed to suffer, facing God's wrath on the cross.

▶ **Read Matthew 26:36-46.**

What feelings did Jesus experience on this night? How do these feelings help us understand the way Jesus relates to us when we suffer?

In both the Old and New Testaments, "cup" is used as a symbol of suffering and God's wrath (Isa. 51:17; Ezek. 23:33; Matt. 20:22). Using this knowledge, summarize Jesus' prayer (v. 39) in your own words.

Compare the difference between Jesus' actions with those of the disciples in the garden.

| Jesus' Actions | Disciples' Actions |
|---|---|
|  |  |

▶ **Read Matthew 6:5-13.**

How do these verses correspond with the way Jesus prayed in the garden?

▶ **Respond**

Jesus knew the disciples desired to stick by His side through anything, but He also knew their flesh would fail them in the difficult days ahead (v. 41). Therefore, He encouraged them to pray.

Describe a time when your spirit was willing but your flesh was weak. What can you learn from that experience?

# PERSONAL STUDY: DAY 5

⭐ **The point: Jesus, God's one and only Son, was forsaken as He bore our sin on the cross.**

Today's passage uses the word "abandoned" to describe Jesus being forsaken by the Father. Other words for this include:

Deserted　　　Rejected　　　Alone　　　Dumped

Forgotten　　　Discarded　　　Dropped　　　Shunned

Highlight a word from the list above you identify with most.

▶ **Read Matthew 27:46.**

While He was on the cross, Jesus not only took on our sin, but also took on God's wrath against our sin. He was the final sacrificial Lamb, separated from God for that moment.

What do you think Jesus meant when He said God had abandoned Him? Why do you think God did this?

Remember, Jesus was abandoned by all of His disciples at His arrest. (See Matt. 26:47-56.) Do you think this added to the pain He endured on the cross? Why or why not?

Why is it important to understand how much Jesus suffered on your behalf? How might understanding the depth of His pain on the cross affect the way we love and serve Him?

▶ **Respond**

Recall a time you felt alone or abandoned. What happened?

List two ways God has comforted you during times when you felt hurt or lonely.

Thank God for the sacrifice of His Son and for Christ's willingness to endure God's wrath and separation from God on our behalf.

# THE RESURRECTION OF JESUS

*JESUS IS THE CENTRAL FOCUS OF SCRIPTURE AND OUR WORSHIP.*

# INTRODUCTION

We all have expectations. We have expectations concerning our families, our friends, our schools and the work we do there, our sports teams or clubs, our small groups, what we want for Christmas and birthdays, God, and so on. Gather students and ask the following:

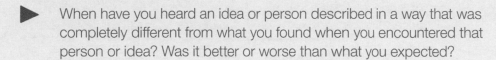 When have you heard an idea or person described in a way that was completely different from what you found when you encountered that person or idea? Was it better or worse than what you expected?

We don't quite know what to expect when our expectations meet reality. Sometimes things are worse than we expected, and sometimes they're better. Jesus' followers expected a conquering leader, the Messiah, but Jesus had died. It was the third day after His death, and they were still expecting something. What would they do next? In the midst of their confusion, Jesus met them (literally) on the road to Emmaus. They didn't recognize Him immediately. He didn't come to them as they expected, but He did come. And with Him being raised from death to life came the offer of a new life for all who believe in Him—one far better than anyone could have ever expected.

# SETTING THE CONTEXT

Jesus was crucified on Good Friday, and so many of the events and details surrounding His crucifixion fulfilled prophecies, as "Hearing the Old Testament in Jesus' Crucifixion" (p. 70) shows. But despite Jesus' repeated warnings of these events, His followers had scattered, worried that they might be next. With evening coming, the Sabbath was about to begin. So Joseph of Arimathea, a wealthy and influential man loyal to Jesus, asked Pilate for Jesus' body and provided a tomb for His quick burial, which the faithful women around Jesus prepared.

Jesus was dead and in the grave, but the Jewish leaders were still nervous. They knew of the prediction that Jesus would rise from the dead, and they were worried that His followers might steal the body and claim He had risen, further perpetuating the notion that Jesus was the Messiah, the Son of God. So the leaders asked Pilate to secure the grave, and the ruler agreed. Pilate assigned a Roman guard to the tomb. These soldiers were sure not to let anyone steal Jesus' body.

# HEARING THE OLD TESTAMENT
## IN JESUS' CRUCIFIXTION

| OLD TESTAMENT | NEW TESTAMENT |
|---|---|
| **Passover**<br>A Lamb's Blood Was Shed to Cover the Israelites' Doorways (Ex. 11–13) | **The Lord's Supper**<br>Jesus' Blood Was Shed to Cover the People's Sins (Matt. 26:26-29) |
| **The Psalmist**<br>Sang of His Suffering at the Hands of Evildoers (Ps. 22:1-18) | **Jesus**<br>Cried Out About His Suffering on the Cross (Matt. 27:35-46) |
| **The Psalmist**<br>Sang of the Lord's Protection over the Bones of the Righteous (Ps. 34:19-20) | **Jesus**<br>Not One of His Bones Was Broken (John 19:31-33,36) |
| **The LORD**<br>They Will Look at Me Whom They Pierced (Zech. 12:10) | **Jesus**<br>A Soldier Pierced His Side with a Spear, Confirming Death (John 19:33-34,37) |
| **Jonah**<br>Three Days and Nights in the Belly of the Fish for His Disobedience (Jonah 1:17) | **Jesus**<br>Three Days and Nights in the Heart of the Earth for Our Salvation (Matt. 12:40) |

# SESSION VIDEOS

Watch this session's video, and then continue the group discussion using the following guide.

▶ What ideas or phrases stood out to you most in the video? Why?

▶ Jesus died for our sins, so why was it essential that He also rise from the dead?

# GROUP DISCUSSION

## As a group, read Luke 24:1-8.

▶ What are some of the emotions the women might have felt?

✪ How would remembering Jesus' predictions of His death and resurrection have helped the women understand what was going on that first Easter?

With the exception of John, the disciples scattered during Jesus' arrest and crucifixion. They were still in hiding on the Sunday morning after the Sabbath. The women, however, had faithfully stood by during Jesus' agonizing hours on the cross, had begun preparing the body for burial, and now were returning to the tomb to finish. They were astonished by what they found—the tomb was open, the guards out of sight, and the body of Jesus gone. Jesus had risen as He promised, but it would take some time before they and the other followers of Jesus would grasp this.

## As a group, read Luke 24:9-12.

▶ What are some of emotions the disciples might have felt?

▶ Why do you think Peter ran to the tomb?

✪ Why did news of Jesus' resurrection come as a shock to so many people?

Peter had to see it for himself. He had followed Jesus to the high priest's house and denied Christ three times. If Christ were raised, then he could see Christ again and perhaps make up for his mistakes. When he got there, Peter marveled at what he saw. The tomb was indeed empty. He may not have understood it in the early morning light, but surely afterward Peter was able to appreciate what God had allowed him to experience: proof that Christ had risen.

**As a group, read Luke 24:13-27.**

▶ Can you relate to these disciples? Have you ever been through an experience only to realize later how God was working in the midst of it?

★ What does Jesus' response to the disciples reveal about the nature and message of the Bible?

Luke highlighted two travelers having a heated discussion about the events of the weekend—the arrest, trial, sentencing, and death of Jesus (v. 20). Jesus' crucifixion had shattered their dreams. And then, Jesus appeared.

Jesus expressed disappointment that the two disciples failed to understand what the Scriptures said. The combination of "foolish" and "slow" suggests they were slow to accept by faith what the Scriptures taught about the Messiah.

The reference to Moses and other prophets referred to the Hebrew Bible—what Christians today refer to as the Old Testament. In Jesus' day, the Old Testament was read as a story in search of a conclusion. The Jewish people in Jesus' day were waiting for the last chapter in their story to begin. Essentially, Jesus said to Cleopas and the other disciple, "I am the one who brings the story to its completion. I am the focus of all the Scriptures."

Our challenge, as disciples of Jesus Christ, is to read the Old Testament Scriptures in light of His death and resurrection. We can do this well by asking three questions every time we read a passage from the Old Testament.

First, ask: Does anything in this passage point directly to Jesus? A few places in the Old Testament speak directly about the coming Messiah, such as Genesis 49:10-12, Isaiah 9:6, and Micah 5:2, to name a few. Of course, direct prophecies of Jesus do not occur in every passage, but you will find them throughout the Old Testament.

Second, ask: Does anything in this passage foreshadow or anticipate Jesus? Sometimes the most powerful way to communicate is through subtlety. In addition to direct prophecies, the Old Testament foreshadows Jesus in subtle, indirect ways. For example, knowing that the Gospel of Matthew begins by identifying Jesus as "the Son of David" and "the Son of Abraham" (Matt. 1:1), we can look for ways that events in David and Abraham's lives anticipate who

Jesus is and what Jesus would do. Abraham's "sacrifice" of Isaac in Genesis 22 foreshadowed the sacrifice of Jesus. Jesus's love for His enemies was indicated by David's love for Mephibosheth—a potential enemy given that he was descendent of King Saul (2 Sam. 9; Rom. 5:8).

Third, ask: How does the gospel of Jesus shape my understanding of this passage? The Old Testament is full of wise sayings, principles, and commands. The Apostle Paul made it clear that these still have relevance for us as followers of Jesus Christ. However, we can only understand how these wise sayings, principles, and commands apply when we read them through the lens of Jesus' life and teaching. He came to bring the Old Testament to its complete expression (Matt. 5:17).

## CHRIST CONNECTION

*On Easter Sunday, God vindicated His Son's perfect sacrifice by raising Him from the dead and beginning the long-promised new creation. Jesus' first followers did not anticipate or believe in the resurrection at first, but the evidence of the resurrection helped grow their faith into full belief. Likewise, through faith, we are united to Christ and share in the promise of being resurrected in His likeness. Sin's curse has been removed, death has been defeated, and we are assured of everlasting life with God.*

# OUR MISSION

 **Head**

Why is it important to not primarily see the Bible as a big book of good behaviors we should live by, but instead as God's story of saving humanity through His Son?

If Jesus makes God known to us, and if the Bible is the best means to learn about Jesus and His teaching, then what is ultimately at stake if we neglect the Scriptures?

 **Heart**

Share about a time when, like the disciples, the Word stirred your heart.

What are some ways you can cultivate a passion and hunger for God's Word in your own life?

🖐 **Hands**

Why was it natural for these two disciples to share the news of Jesus' resurrection?

What can help our evangelism feel more natural?

# PERSONAL STUDY: DAY 1

⭐ **The point: Jesus' empty tomb visibly proved His resurrection.**

▶ **Read Matthew 28:1-6.**

Much like we take flowers to a grave today, these women were going to pay respect to Jesus. Do you think the two Marys were expecting to see anything out of the ordinary? Why or why not?

What emotions do you think these women experienced as they approached the tomb?

In your own words, explain the angel's message.

The women were _____ when they first saw the angel. How do you think the women's feelings changed as they heard the angel's message? Explain.

How does the reality of the angel's message bring joy instead of fear?

▶ **Respond**

Imagine you were with the Marys on their journey to the tomb. In your journal, describe how you would have felt, questions you would have had, and how you would have responded to Jesus being "gone."

Answer the question, "What does the empty tomb mean to me?"

For further study on the women who were devoted to Jesus, read Mark 15:40,47; 16:1.

⭐ **The point: The empty tomb is cause for worship.**

▶ **Read Matthew 28:7-9.**

In your own words, record the command the angel gave the women.

How did the women respond to the angel's command?

What can you learn from the obedience of these women?

What happened when these women encountered Jesus?

How do you think their encounter with Jesus fueled them to complete their mission?

▶ **Respond**

In your journal, finish these statements:

• I first believed the resurrection of Jesus when …

• My belief in the resurrection changes me because …

The women responded quickly and worshipfully. When you encounter Jesus, how do you respond? How might an apathetic response indicate something is missing in your personal worship?

For further study on why Jesus' resurrection is praiseworthy, read 1 Peter 1:3-4.

# PERSONAL STUDY: DAY 3

⭐ **The point: The Risen King comes to His people when they are confused and disheartened.**

▶ **Read Luke 24:13-24.**

The travellers are having an intense dispute (v. 15,17) over the One they hoped would "redeem Israel" (v. 21). The Jews hoped for a ruler to overthrow Roman power, but Jesus had died. How did their expectations fuel their discouragement and confusion?

Why do you think they were prevented from recognizing Jesus?

What was their reaction to the news from those who visited Jesus' empty tomb?

▶ **Respond**

The disciples on the Emmaus road were sad and confused. Jesus didn't immediately reveal Himself to them, but He walked alongside them and joined their discussion.

Describe a time in your life when you were discouraged and confused. How did Jesus walk alongside you during that time? How did He encourage you?

Read Romans 8:31-39 and list two or three thoughts on an index card to help you whenever you're confused or discouraged.

## ✪ The point: The Bible's focus is on Jesus, the Risen King.

We all can tell stories of unclear situations that later became clear. Describe a time when you were confused about something in the moment that later made sense.

▶ **Read Luke 24:25-27.**

Some disciples were called hardhearted because they would not believe those who saw Jesus after His resurrection (Mark 16:14). What similar words did Jesus say to them in verse 25?

When Jesus called these disciples "foolish" and "slow," He wasn't insulting their intelligence, but chastising their lack of faith in His Word. He drew their attention to evidence from the Old Testament that pointed to the way He would suffer and die (Isa. 53:1-9).

What does this say about the message of God's Word and the importance of understanding and faithfully believing that message?

Who is the focus of the Bible's message? Why is it important for us to remember this every day?

Why do you think we're often "slow" and "foolish" when it comes to our faith?

▶ **Respond**

Like the disciples, we can be slow to make connections between the Scripture and our lives. Pray and ask God to open your eyes to the connections within Scripture, and then dedicate more time to studying the Bible in order to not only understand these connections, but to hide them within your heart.

# PERSONAL STUDY: DAY 5

⭐ **The point: Jesus reveals Himself to His people.**

▶ **Read Luke 24:28-35.**

Why do you think the disciples invited Jesus to stay with them?

Highlight the word "then" in verse 31. What happened to open the disciples' eyes?

Think back to yesterday's devotion. Jesus had prevented the same disciples from recognizing Him. In this passage, He opened their eyes. Why do you think He waited to allow them to see who He really was?

In your own words, describe the disciples' response to Jesus' revelation. How would you have responded?

▶ **Respond**

On a scale of 1 to 10, how open are you to hearing God's voice through the Scriptures?

List a few things that might compete with your attention as you try to really dig into Scripture and see the greater story, God's story, throughout the Bible. Then, ask God to help you stay focused and to see what He reveals to you.

# THE COMMISSION FROM JESUS

*JESUS CALLS ALL OF HIS FOLLOWERS TO
GO AND MAKE DISCIPLES.*

# INTRODUCTION

Jesus has called all of His disciples—including us—to go and make disciples. Sometimes the command to "go" means that Jesus will ask us to pick up everything and go across the world to tell others about Him. Not all of us are called to go to a foreign country, but we are all called to reach out to every person we meet—the people around us, in the places we "go" all the time.

▶ Where are some places you "go"?

▶ How can you make disciples in those places?

People often face the temptation to only reach out to people who are like them, who are already their friends, or who go to the same school or church. But we should reach out to people we don't always talk to or know well, even if that feels uncomfortable at first. It's important to remember that Jesus made no exceptions in His command about who we should "go" to, and neither should we.

# SETTING THE CONTEXT

Christ had risen from the dead. He had appeared to many of His followers in the days after He came out of the tomb to provide them evidence and encouragement they needed. He appeared to the women and the travelers on the road to Emmaus.

He appeared to the disciples all together in a locked room because they were still living in fear of the Jewish leaders (the locked door was no barrier for Jesus). Because Thomas was not among them and responded with doubt to the other disciples, the scene repeated itself about a week later. Thomas no longer doubted but worshiped Jesus—"My Lord and my God!" (John 20:28). He and the disciples began to understand Jesus' identity as God.

The apostle Paul would later write that Jesus appeared to some five hundred disciples at the same time, providing an overwhelming testimony to the validity of His resurrection. Jesus was—and is—alive. And He has work for His followers to do—to proclaim the gospel on account of "Jesus' Exaltation" (p. 82).

# JESUS' EXALTATION

| JESUS' EXALTATION | RESPOND IN FAITH | RESPOND IN WORSHIP AND MISSIONS |
|---|---|---|
| The Messiah Was Raised from the Dead (Matt. 28:5-6) | Blessed are those who believe in Jesus' resurrection, even without seeing Him (John 20:27,29) | Praise to "my Lord and my God" (John 20:28)<br><br>Call people to repentance because one day Jesus will judge the world (Acts 17:30-31) |
| The Risen King Was Given All Authority in Heaven and on Earth (Matt. 28:18) | Confess with your mouth that Jesus is Lord and believe in your heart that God raised Him from the dead and you will be saved (Rom. 10:9) | Go and make disciples of all nations, baptizing them in the name of the Father, Son, and Holy Spirit, and teaching them to observe everything Jesus commanded (Matt. 28:19-20) |
| The Risen King Ascended into Heaven (Acts 1:9-11; 2:33-36) | Repent and be baptized in Jesus' name for the forgiveness of sins, and you will receive the promised Holy Spirit (Acts 2:38) | Set your minds on things above, where Christ is seated (Col. 3:1-17)<br><br>Use your gifts from Jesus through the Holy Spirit to serve others (1 Pet. 4:10-11) |
| Jesus Will Come Again on the Final "Day of the Lord" (Rev. 19–22) | While doing what is good, entrust yourself to a faithful Creator and Savior (1 Pet. 4:17-19) | While looking forward to Christ's appearance, proclaim the gospel, endure hardship, do the work of an evangelist, and one day receive from the Lord the crown of righteousness (2 Tim. 4:1-8) |

# SESSION VIDEOS

Watch this session's video, and then continue the group discussion using the following guide.

▶ What ideas or phrases stood out to you most in the video? Why?

▶ Why do you think Jesus appeared to so many people after His resurrection?

# GROUP DISCUSSION

**As a group, read Matthew 28:16-20.**

▶ Why did Jesus begin His commission with a statement of His authority?

▶ What are the key parts of Jesus' commission?

★ How do worship and mission relate to one another?

Jesus' disciples needed to understand the importance of His authority over all things, and this is still important for us to understand today. The reality of His power and authority didn't end with His resurrection or ascension or at the writing of the biblical text. Jesus' kingdom and His authority are eternal. Jesus began this commission with the statement of His authority and then connected it to the command to "go," indicating that the power that raised Jesus from the dead and seated Him by the throne of grace is the same power available to us to live out this call to go and make disciples of all nations.

The disciples were instructed to go (Matt. 28:19). This was not a suggestion. Jesus wasn't telling the disciples that maybe they should go, or they could go if they could squeeze it into their schedules. Jesus used an imperative, a command, an order to be obeyed. Jesus, the risen King, commanded them to go.

"Go" in this passage is a verb that means to travel or journey, and the disciples were expected to obey. Our temptation and theirs would be to wait, but in essence, Jesus said, "Now that you've heard of My authority and seen My power—even over death—go out into the world and let others know of this good news for the forgiveness of sins."

But where do we go? Since Jesus has authority over all the earth, He commands His disciples to go to all nations. Every tribe, tongue, and nation is under Jesus' authority, even if they have not yet submitted their lives to Him. After all, we have been told that one day every knee shall bow and every tongue confess that Jesus is Lord at the mention of His name (Phil. 2:10-11). So, we go.

# GROUP DISCUSSION *CONT.*

For the disciples, going meant being scattered among the peoples and nations of the world, and for many of us, it means the same. Jesus' call is for a multi-ethnic, cross-cultural focus of missionaries that may require leaving home and the familiar to travel into foreign lands of the unknown. But the Lord didn't tell us here exactly where to go. He didn't demand that we all leave home; He simply said to go and make disciples of all nations.

### As a group, read Acts 1:4-8.

⭐ Why was it essential for the disciples to wait for the Holy Spirit before embarking on the mission Jesus had given?

▶ What does it mean to be Jesus' witness? What are we witnesses to?

Jesus had given His followers a mission, and that mission was essential. But they lacked one thing that was essential to complete that mission—power. They would not be able to fulfill it. They needed power from outside of themselves, power from God. That is why they needed to wait for the Holy Spirit. Without the Spirit, there is no power. The Spirit is the energy that enables believers to overcome their fears and to fulfill what their Master has commanded them to do—to be His witnesses. A witness is someone who has seen or experienced something and then tells others about it. In Christianity, a witness is someone who has experienced Jesus Christ through the gospel and then tells the unbelieving world about Him.

### As a group, read Acts 1:9-11.

⭐ What was the significance of Jesus' ascension into heaven?

▶ What does this teach us about Christ's future coming?

The angels confirmed that Jesus, who was taken from them, would come back in the same way: visibly, bodily, and with the clouds of glory. For now, Jesus was returning to the place of glory He had left next to the Father. But although Jesus was gone, the disciples were to be busy with His commission. This was a mandate for all, including believers today, to stop gazing and get to work being on mission with God.

## CHRIST CONNECTION

*Before Jesus ascended to the Father, He commissioned His disciples to go into the world and make disciples of all nations. Under the authority of Jesus and with the power of the Holy Spirit, we make disciples of all peoples as we anticipate the return of Christ.*

# OUR MISSION

 **Head**

How have you experienced discipleship from a mature believer in your own life?

How can we encourage one another toward making disciples?

 **Heart**

What are some ways we can unintentionally make the message of the gospel about us instead of about Jesus?

How does Jesus' authority help us when we feel fearful?

**Hands**

What places have you gone in order to share the gospel and make disciples?

How can your group/church work together and support one another in this shared mission to go and make disciples of all nations?

# PERSONAL STUDY: DAY 1

⭐ **The point: Jesus commissioned His disciples to go and share the gospel under His authority.**

▶ **Read Matthew 28:16-18.**

The disciples went to _____, because _____ had _____ them there.

Why is this significant in regard to our mission as Christ-followers?

How would you describe the reactions of those who met here with Jesus?

How did Jesus respond to His people when He met with them? How can this encourage us in our ministry today?

Jesus wasn't shaken by His disciples' unbelief and isn't shaken by ours. However, He did remind them of what was at stake and presented His mission and expectations to them.

Underline the words "all authority" in your Bible. Who gave Jesus this authority? Why is it important for us to know this?

What does that authority imply for our mission?

▶ **Respond**

Some of Jesus' disciples were doubtful, so Jesus answered their doubts. Have you ever doubted? Does it comfort you to know that God has ultimate authority?

On an index card, write a short prayer responding to Jesus' authority, care for His people, and the commission of His followers.

⭐ **The point: Jesus commissioned His followers to make disciples through sharing the gospel.**

▶ **Read Matthew 28:19.**

List the three commands Jesus gave His disciples in this verse. Then, briefly describe what each action means or implies.

Jesus had just told His disciples that He had "all authority" (Matt. 28:18). What does this have to do with the word "therefore" in today's Scripture?

Were any specific nations mentioned in this verse? What does this tell us about God?

Sometimes God calls people to go to foreign countries to share the gospel, but all of us can be on mission as we go live life each day.

How can believers encourage one another to make disciples, no matter where we go?

▶ **Respond**

Look back to the three commands in this verse. Jot down one way you can obey each of these commands today.

Take a moment to reflect: Have I ever shared the gospel with another person? How did I share? What was the result?

Often fear or pride keeps us from obeying Christ's commission. What fears have tempted you to ignore God's commands? Confess any fears and ask God for help.

# PERSONAL STUDY: DAY 3

⭐ **The point: Jesus commissioned His disciples to disciple others.**

▶ **Read Matthew 28:20.**

What did Jesus want His disciples to teach?

Look through the New Testament and list some of the commands Jesus gave to His disciples.

Why is it important for Christ-followers to teach each other about Jesus? Why are we sometimes afraid to do so?

Highlight the promise in the last half of this verse. Why do you think Matthew closed his Gospel with these words? Why do you think it's important to remember Jesus is always with us?

▶ **Respond**

We are God's ambassadors to the world around us (2 Cor. 5:20). We must live out the gospel, no matter where we are or who's around us. Consider your relationships. Ask yourself: Do I change depending on who's around me?

How have you experienced discipleship in your life? How has this impacted your walk with God?

Ask God to reveal to you who He wants you to disciple or teach. Commit to obeying Him by reaching out to that person when He gives you the opportunity.

## ★ The point: Jesus promised to send the Holy Spirit to empower His disciples.

What are some promises people have made to you and failed to deliver? How does this experience affect the way you see God's promises? Explain.

### ▶ Read Acts 1:4-5.

What was "the Father's promise" (v. 4) that Jesus instructed the disciples to wait for?

Why was this promise so important to the disciples? Why is it so important to us today?

Many times, waiting on God can lead to doubt. What are some things that can get in the way of you trusting God's promises?

### ▶ Respond

What are some promises from God that you struggle sometimes to believe in? Develop three ways that you can overcome this lack of faith and how you can respond when you are faced with these feelings.

Thank God for sending the gift of the Holy Spirit to those who trust in Him.

# PERSONAL STUDY: DAY 5

⭐ **The point: Jesus foretold the spread of the gospel message.**

What comes to mind when you hear the word *mystery*? What is the first step you take when faced with something you don't understand?

▶ **Read Acts 1:6-8.**

Jesus knew the disciples could not know everything about His plans and His timing. Where did He direct their focus instead?

How can we learn from Jesus' response to His disciples' question about timing?

Jesus promised the disciples would not go alone; rather they would go in and with the power of the Holy Spirit. In what other examples throughout Scripture do you see the Holy Spirit at work empowering and comforting?

How does the reality of the Holy Spirit impact you as you carry out the Great Commission?

▶ **Respond**

Although Jesus did not tell the disciples everything, He told them what they needed to know to fulfill their purpose of carrying on the gospel message.

List some situations or circumstances in your life for which you still seek answers. (Maybe this is knowing God's plan for your life or how He is working behind the scenes for you.)

Ask God to help you trust Him even when you don't have all the answers.

# HOW TO USE THE LEADER GUIDE

## Prepare to Lead

The Leader Guide is designed to be cut out along the dotted line so you, the leader, can have this front-and-back page with you as you lead your group through the session.

*Watch the session video* and *read through the session content* with the Leader Guide cut-out in hand and notice how it supplements each section of the study.

Use the *Session Objective* in the Leader Guide to help focus your preparation and leadership in the group session.

## Questions & Answers

⭐ Questions in the session content with this icon have some sample answers provided in the Leader Guide, if needed, to help you jump-start or steer the conversation.

## Setting the Context

This section of the session always has an *infographic* on the opposite page. The Leader Guide provides an activity to help your group members interact with the content communicated through the infographic.

## Group Discussion

The Group Discussion contains the main teaching content for each session, providing questions for students to interact with as you move through the biblical passages. Some of these questions will have suggested answers in the Leader Guide.

## Our Mission ⭕ ✔ ✋

The Our Mission is a summary application section designed to highlight how the biblical passages being studied challenge the way we think, feel, and live today. Some of these questions will have suggested answers in the Leader Guide.

## Pray

Conclude each group session with a prayer. A brief sample prayer is provided at the end of each Leader Guide cut-out.

## Session Objective

Show that the birth of Jesus was the fulfillment of what the Old Testament pointed to and that He is the One Israel and the world have waited for.

## Introducing the Study

Use this intro to set the context for the birth of Jesus, the promised Messiah.

## Setting the Context

Use the following activity to help group members see the significance of a Christ-centered reading of Scripture.

Encourage group members to look through the connections on "Hearing the Old Testament in Jesus' Birth" (p. 10). Then ask the following questions: "Which fulfillment of Old Testament prophecy stands out to you the most? Why?" "Why does it matter that Jesus came as a descendant of Abraham and David?" "What is significant about prophecies regarding Jesus being delivered during the times of the prophets and kings?"

Read this paragraph to transition to the next part of the study.

The Bible, from beginning to end, is the story of God's work in the world, and His work has always been centered on the person and work of Jesus Christ, God's Son. Our study of the Old Testament up to this point has been pointing to and preparing the way for the coming of Jesus so that we will recognize Him and believe in Him for eternal life.

## Group Discussion

Watch this session's video, and then as part of the group discussion, use these answers as needed for the questions highlighted in this section.

⭐ Why is it important to see Jesus as the fulfillment of God's promises in the Old Testament? *1) So we know for certain Jesus was the One God sent to save us from our sin. 2) So we can proclaim to the world the truth about Jesus with confidence and boldness. 3) So we can again see that God is indeed the promise-keeping God He has always been.*

⭐ How was Jesus' birth related to God's promise to Abraham? *1) God promised Abraham an offspring through whom would come the blessing to the world; Jesus is that offspring. 2) The promised land to Abraham and his descendants will find its ultimate fulfillment in the worldwide and eternal reign of Jesus as King over His people. 3) God promised to bless Abraham and his descendants; Jesus is the ultimate blessing for God's people.*

⭐ What does the setting of Jesus' birth tell us about God's intent in sending Him? *1) Being born in the city of David, Jesus was to fulfill God's promise to David of an eternal king. 2) Jesus' humble birthplace meant He would identify with the poor, the lowly, and the humble and bring salvation to all who humble themselves. 3) Jesus did not come to be served but to serve others; He came not in pride but in humility.*

## Our Mission

⭕ How does Mary's faith as a young teenager encourage you in your own obedience to God? *The image of the great angel Gabriel appearing to a marginalized teenager in an insignificant and impoverished village like Nazareth establishes a contrast that Luke maintained throughout his Gospel. Earlier in the story, Gabriel was forced to explain his identity to the unbelieving priest in the holy place (Luke 1:19). Zechariah questioned the truth of Gabriel's words, despite Gabriel's declaration that he stood in the presence of God (Luke 1:18). But Gabriel found a more faithful person in Mary. She also asked how Gabriel's message could be, but hers was more a question of process than disbelief. Luke intended for us to appreciate the contrast between the disbelieving priest in the magnificent temple and the trusting girl in impoverished Nazareth.*

✋ In what ways has your relationship with Jesus changed your own life? *The shepherds left the manger scene eager to tell others what they had experienced. This is how people responded when they met Jesus and understood who He was. The same response must be true for those of us who meet Christ, as well. Like the shepherds, we will naturally tell of God's goodness to others once we have embraced the good news of what God has done in our own lives. We do not share begrudgingly or out of a sense of duty, but from a heartfelt delight as a result of knowing that our sins have been forgiven.*

## Pray

Close your group in prayer, thanking God for His willingness to humble Himself in Christ to come to us.

# SESSION 2 · LEADER GUIDE

## Session Objective

Show that God prepared Jesus for His earthly ministry through John the Baptist's ministry as a messenger and also through His baptism and temptation in the wilderness. Where Adam and Israel failed, Jesus succeeded, proving He is the sinless Savior we need.

## Introducing the Study

Use this intro to set the context for Jesus' temptation in the wilderness.

## Setting the Context

Use the following activity to help group members see the importance of Jesus' being both fully God and fully man.

Call attention to "Jesus Is God" (p. 22) and ask group members to identify the points related to Jesus' childhood. Then encourage them to marvel at the thought of the preexistent Son of God taking on flesh and living as a little child within His creation. Ask the following questions: "What are some questions raised by the Son of God taking on flesh?" "What might it mean that Scripture does not tease out for us all the implications of Jesus' deity and humanity?" "How does Jesus' being fully human teach us about what it means to be a human being made in the image of God?"

Read this paragraph to transition to the next part of the study.

The divine and human natures of Jesus are vitally important for the work that He came to earth to do, and the preparation of Jesus in His baptism and wilderness temptation reflect the significance of His two natures. We must never forget that Jesus is both fully God and fully man.

## Group Discussion

Watch this session's video, and then as part of the group discussion, use these answers as needed for the questions highlighted in this section.

★ How would you explain repentance to a non-Christian? *1) Repentance is changing your mind about your sin; what you once desired to do as a violation of God's law you now reject in favor of doing what God wants you to do. 2) Repentance is changing the direction of your life; heading down the broad road leading to destruction, repenting means turning around and following the narrow path of Jesus that leads to life.*

★ Why was Jesus baptized even though He didn't need to repent of sin? *1) Jesus came to be like us in every way, except without sin, so He was baptized in order to identify Himself with the repentant sinners He came to save. 2) Jesus' baptism affirmed the ministry and message of John the Baptist. 3) Jesus' baptism was a step of obedience to God the Father, as demonstrated by His affirmation of Jesus from the heavens.*

★ How was the temptation of Jesus similar to and different from the temptation Adam and Eve experienced in the garden? *1) They were both tempted regarding food. 2) They were both tempted regarding the nature of deity. 3) Adam and Eve doubted God's word, whereas Jesus trusted in God's word completely, even using it as a weapon of defense against Satan's temptations.*

## Our Mission

○ How does this account change the way you view difficult times in your life? What are some important lessons we can learn through times like these? *The wilderness is the place God uses to establish our identity as His sons and daughters. In the Old Testament, God called His people to the wilderness so they could learn His worth and learn to truly worship Him. Pharaoh was told to let the people go to the wilderness to worship God. In the wilderness, Israel learned the words of God. The same can be said of the wilderness temptation of Jesus. Jesus' sonship was declared by the Father at the Jordan River, and His relationship with the Father was strengthened by His obedience in the wilderness. There Jesus demonstrated what it truly means to be a child of God.*

## Pray

Close your group in prayer, thanking God that His Word is trustworthy and true.

# SESSION 3 · LEADER GUIDE

## Session Objective

Show that all of Jesus' miracles were designed to reveal His identity and support His teachings, as they also flowed from His deep compassion for people.

## Introducing the Study

Use this intro to set the context for a discussion about Jesus' miracles.

## Setting the Context

Use the following activity to help group members see the purpose of Jesus' miracles.

Ask group members to name some signs they see on a regular basis (signs for businesses; billboards; traffic signs; etc.). Then ask what is the purpose of these signs (to get attention; to draw you in; to provide direction and instruction). Let group members review the seven miracles on "Jesus' Signs in the Gospel of John" (p. 34) and ask the following questions: "Why do you think John chose to call these miracles 'signs'?" "How do the various responses to Jesus' signs relate to the responses people have to signs in our day?" Conclude this activity by reading John 20:30-31, which gives John's reason for recording these signs in his Gospel: "Jesus performed many other signs in the presence of his disciples that are not written in this book. But these are written so that you may believe that Jesus is the Messiah, the Son of God, and that by believing you may have life in his name."

## Group Discussion

Watch this session's video, and then as part of the group discussion, use these answers as needed for the questions highlighted in this section.

⭐ Why were the miracles of Jesus essential to His authority? *1) They supported the power of His gospel message and teaching. 2) They confirmed His authority over both the physical and spiritual realms. 3) They validated His ministry as the promised Messiah.*

⭐ What can we learn about how Jesus viewed His mission from these verses? *1) Jesus was not concerned with popularity or fame; these were not integral to His mission. 2) Jesus' mission was not primarily about miracles but about the message of repentance and faith. 3) Jesus wanted as many people as possible to hear the gospel message.*

⭐ Why is it significant that Jesus was moved to compassion and reached out and touched the man? *1) It is powerful to consider that the God of all the universe is moved with compassion by the plight of His image bearers and their faith. 2) Jesus is the image of God, the full revelation of God's character, and this scene of Jesus' compassion and miracle-working power combats the way the world often sees God. 3) Touching a leper made one unclean, but in this case, the purity of Jesus went the other way and washed this leper clean of his uncleanness.*

## Our Mission

○ What is the danger in seeking Jesus because of what we think He might be able to do for us? *Jesus' focus on His God-given mission reminds us to examine why we seek after Jesus. Are we, like the crowds at Capernaum, coming to Him because of what we think He can do for us? Are we looking to Him to change our current circumstances? Or have we recognized the true identity of the Son of God and come to Him in submission—in worship with gratitude for what He has already done for us?*

## Pray

Close your group in prayer, thanking God that Jesus is not put off by our sin but, in His compassion, is willing to come near to us.

# SESSION 4 • LEADER GUIDE

## Session Objective

Show from this parable that Jesus came to bring all kinds of sinners to repentance and that His teachings all centered on this purpose—how we can be right with God through Him.

## Introducing the Study

Use this intro as a way to set up the scene and context of Jesus' parable of the prodigal sons.

## Setting the Context

Use the following activity to help group members see the spiritual aspect of Jesus' parables.

Ask group members what some of their favorite stories are and what they have meant to them. Explain that we find meaning in stories because that is how God made us, but understanding the proper spiritual significance of Jesus' parables apart from faith in Him is impossible because true understanding leads to faith-filled response—it leads to repentance, faith, and obedience.

Allow group members to look over the information on "Parables of the Kingdom" (p. 46). Then ask the following questions: "What are some ways Christians need to respond to the parables Jesus told about the kingdom of God?" "How are these responses different from the ways of this world?"

## Group Discussion

Watch this session's video, and then as part of the group discussion, use these answers as needed for the questions highlighted in this section.

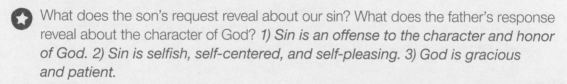 What does the son's request reveal about our sin? What does the father's response reveal about the character of God? *1) Sin is an offense to the character and honor of God. 2) Sin is selfish, self-centered, and self-pleasing. 3) God is gracious and patient.*

⭐ Where do you see the gospel in his response? *1) Heaven celebrates when even one sinner repents of his or her sin (Luke 15:7,10). 2) God's gift of salvation takes an enemy of God and creates a son or daughter of God. 3) God does not keep a record of wrongs with His children but welcomes them home when they repent and return to Him.*

⭐ What does this interaction with his father reveal about how the older son sees himself? *1) The older brother sees himself as a slave of the father, working to earn his good favor. 2) The older son sees himself as righteous and worthy because he is better than his brother. 3) He sees himself as a dutiful and obedient son.*

## Our Mission

🔻 Why does a heart closed off to God lead to a refusal to accept repentant sinners? *Jesus' parable describes two types of sin—the outward rebellion exposed in the younger son and the inward bitterness concealed in the older son. The gracious father responded to both of his children with honor and love. But unlike the younger son, who fell with tears of repentance into his father's arms, the older son simply voiced a whiny complaint. His boasting about his faithful service revealed that he saw his father as if he were only a boss to be obeyed, and he was convinced he had been treated wrongly. How people respond when someone outside the church becomes a believer says a lot about their own hearts. For instance, those who have experienced the grace of God in Christ will gladly rejoice when other sinners experience that grace as well. It is the same principle of forgiving because you have been forgiven or showing compassion because you have been shown compassion. However, a heart closed-off to God will clearly reveal itself in the way one relates to sinners in need of grace.*

✋ In what ways does wasting God's gifts lead to slavery instead of freedom? *One thing we learn from the younger son is that outwardly-rebellious sin eventually leads people to squander away their lives until they are at the mercy of whatever they have glued themselves to. People attach themselves to drugs, alcohol, relationships, TV, and so forth. We become addicted to something or someone we think will provide hope; instead, the addiction brings enslavement, reminding us to daily avoid the temptation to fall into the traps of the older brother and the younger brother.*

## Pray

Close your group in prayer, thanking God that He always welcomes us with open arms of forgiveness when we repent of our sin and turn to Him in faith.

# SESSION 5 · LEADER GUIDE

## Session Objective

Show that the crucifixion is the apex of the story of Scripture and that only through Jesus' death can we be saved from our sin.

## Introducing the Study

Use this intro as a way to begin the session on Jesus' crucifixion.

## Setting the Context

Use the following activity to help group members see what the crucifixion means for the followers of Jesus.

Encourage group members to read over "Jesus' Suffering" (p. 58) and to feel the weight of the suffering Jesus experienced for our sake. Ask the group to identify what distinguishes the red and blue rows. Use the following to help explain the differences.

• Red Rows: Jesus' physical suffering at the hands of human beings. Those who are Jesus' disciples are expected to take up their cross of suffering and follow Him, even though that may mean betrayal, physical suffering, and even death for the sake of Jesus' name.

• Blue Rows: Jesus' experience of suffering the wrath of God against sin. While Jesus' followers should expect suffering at the hands of human beings, they will never experience the wrath of God because Jesus has taken that in their place to save them from sin and its eternal consequences.

Ask the following question: "How do the blue rows encourage you, even with the expectation of suffering found in the red rows?"

## Group Discussion

Watch this session's video, and then as part of the group discussion, use these answers as needed for the questions highlighted in this section.

⭐ How did Jesus give new meaning to the Passover celebration? *1) The Lord's Supper superseded the Passover meal as a remembrance of the greater exodus for God's people from slavery to sin. 2) The blood of the Passover lamb pointed forward to the blood of Jesus. 3) The Passover was celebrated by families, but the Lord's Supper is celebrated by churches comprised of people from every tribe, language, and nation.*

⭐ How does this garden scene compare with the first garden scene in the Bible—the garden of Eden? What temptations were presented in both? *1) Adam and Eve succumbed to their temptation, but Jesus struggled mightily against temptation and prevailed. 2) Adam and Eve desired to be like God, but Jesus, who is God, humbled Himself to obey the Father and die for humanity. 3) Adam's sin brought death upon humanity; according to God's will, Jesus resolved to take that death upon Himself in order to bring life to humanity.*

⭐ Why is it significant that the curtain was ripped, and ripped from top to bottom? *1) The curtain barred access to the most holy place, where God was said to dwell in the temple in His holiness. 2) The curtain was ripped from top to bottom, indicating that this was the work of God opening up access to His presence through the death of Jesus. 3) No longer was the most holy place restricted to the high priest, but now God's holy presence is available to all because of Jesus' sacrifice.*

## Our Mission

❤ What would it look like for a Christian to yearn for the consummation of the kingdom? *The message of the coming kingdom is a message of hope and joy and fulfillment. It is the longing of the Christian heart. This is why we pray, "Your kingdom come" (Matt. 6:10). We anticipate the day when wars and violence cease and when peace reigns. We yearn for the day when sin's teeth have ceased biting and death itself is dead. We hunger and thirst for the kingdom because we hunger and thirst for the King of righteousness, and we will be with Him then and there.*

## Pray

Close your group in prayer, praising God for providing Jesus as a sacrifice for our sins and thanking Him for the freedom that comes through that sacrifice.

## Session Objective

Show that the resurrection was difficult for the first disciples to believe, but they had been given all they needed—both prophecy and proof—to recognize that Jesus was crucified and raised on the third day.

## Introducing the Study

Use this intro to set the scene for a discussion on the resurrection of Jesus.

## Setting the Context

Use the following activity to help group members see how Jesus' crucifixion and resurrection relate to one another.

Direct group members to look at the connections on "Hearing the Old Testament in Jesus' Crucifixion" (p. 70). Then ask the following questions: "Why do you think there are so many explicit prophecies relating to Jesus' crucifixion?" "What is the relationship between Jesus' crucifixion and resurrection? Is one more important than the other? Why or why not?"

Explain that regarding Jesus' crucifixion and resurrection, we cannot have one without the other—they are both equally and vitally important. The crucifixion of Jesus would mean nothing without His resurrection; we would still be dead in our sins. And there is certainly no need for a resurrection if Jesus was not crucified, in which case we are also still dead in our sins. We believe in and serve a crucified and risen Savior. Anything less is not the Jesus of the Bible.

## Group Discussion

Watch this session's video, and then as part of the group discussion, use these answers as needed for the questions highlighted in this section.

⭐ How would remembering Jesus' predictions of His death and resurrection have helped the women understand what was going on that first Easter? *1) Jesus said He would be crucified and He was—He always spoke the truth. 2) Because Jesus predicted His crucifixion, they could have also believed His prediction of His resurrection. 3) Jesus' predictions would have recalled the words of the prophets that addressed the suffering and resurrection of the Messiah.*

⭐ Why did news of Jesus' resurrection come as a shock to so many people? *1) It sounded like nonsense; yes, He raised others from the dead, but could He raise Himself? 2) Because they failed to believe all that the Scriptures had said regarding the Messiah. 3) Because our sinful hearts make it hard to believe God can do the impossible.*

⭐ What does Jesus' response to the disciples reveal about the nature and message of the Bible? *1) The Bible is clear that the Messiah would suffer and rise again. 2) Though the books of the Bible have been written by numerous authors, there is one Author—God Himself—who has inspired every word so the whole story points to Jesus. 3) In our sin, we miss the point of Scripture; only with the wisdom of God through the Holy Spirit can we rightly discern Scripture and obey it.*

## Our Mission

❤ What are some ways you can cultivate a passion and hunger for God's Word in your own life? *These disciples rightly captured what happens when we correctly understand the Bible when they said, "'Weren't our hearts burning within us while he was talking with us on the road and explaining the Scriptures to us?'" (Luke 24:32). For the disciples and countless Christians over the centuries, understanding the Bible and seeing how all of the stories and events point to Jesus sets our hearts on fire, creating a love and passion for the Word and a hunger for more of it.*

✋ Why was it natural for these two disciples to share the news of Jesus' resurrection? *Note how the disciples on the road to Emmaus quickly went to share the good news of Jesus' resurrection. An encounter with Jesus is not meant to be kept secret. It leads to mission. When Jesus reveals Himself to us, He expects us to spread His glory and fame through our witness to others.*

## Pray

Close your group in prayer, thanking God for the unique hope we have as Christians because of the resurrection of Jesus.

# SESSION 7 · LEADER GUIDE

## Session Objective

Show that Jesus gave His followers clear instructions for how they were to make disciples of all the nations through the power of the Holy Spirit as they work and wait for His return.

## Introducing the Study

Use this section to introduce the biblical concept of the Great Commission.

## Setting the Context

Use the following activity to help group members see the importance of Jesus' exaltation in His crucifixion, resurrection, and ascension.

Call attention to "Jesus' Exaltation" (p. 82) and ask the following questions:

• What does exaltation mean? *To be lifted up, elevated.*

• What exaltation of Jesus could be missing from this list? *Jesus' crucifixion [see John 12:32-33].*

• How does Jesus embody the biblical principle that God opposes the proud but gives grace to the humble (Prov. 3:34; Jas. 4:6; 1 Pet. 5:5)? *The Son of God humbled Himself to take on flesh and die in the place of sinners, so God raised Him up from the dead and to His throne, and every knee will bow to Him and every tongue confess that He is Lord [see Phil. 2:5-11].*

## Group Discussion

Watch this session's video, and then as part of the group discussion, use these answers as needed for the questions highlighted in this section.

⭐ How do worship and mission relate to one another? *1) Those who worship Jesus will feel compelled to live on mission for Him. 2) The mission seeks to make more worshipers of Jesus Christ. 3) If Jesus is not God, then He is not worthy of our worship, nor is He worthy of the gospel mission.*

⭐ Why was it essential for the disciples to wait for the Holy Spirit before embarking on the mission Jesus had given? *1) So they had power and boldness to proclaim the gospel to a hostile world. 2) So they had wisdom and the words to say when addressing all sorts of people with the gospel. 3) So they knew Jesus was with them as they fulfilled the Great Commission.*

⭐ What was the significance of Jesus' ascension into heaven? *1) Jesus was returning back to the Father, where He sat down at His right hand to rule over all creation. 2) Jesus' ascension in the clouds fulfilled Daniel's vision of "one like a son of man" being given an eternal kingdom (Dan. 7:13-14). 3) Christians on mission serve as ambassadors of the King over all the universe, proclaiming His gospel, greatness, and praise so people will join His kingdom through repentance and faith.*

## Our Mission

🔻 How does Jesus' authority help us when we feel fearful? *Our temptation not to share with others is often rooted in fear: What should I say? What if they won't accept me? How will I look in their eyes? What if the response is violence? When Jesus is the focus and the message, we can rest from our fear. We don't need to fear human beings because, Jesus instructed: "Don't fear those who kill the body but are not able to kill the soul; rather, fear him who is able to destroy both soul and body in hell" (Matt. 10:28).*

## Pray

Close your group in prayer, praying that you would be busy about the work God has given you to as a follower of Christ.

# A NEW BEGINNING...

The good news of God's saving grace spreads as God's followers obey the call to create disciples of all nations.